Herbert Probert

**Life and Scenes in Congo**

Vol. 1

Herbert Probert

**Life and Scenes in Congo**
*Vol. 1*

ISBN/EAN: 9783337240080

Printed in Europe, USA, Canada, Australia, Japan

Cover: Foto ©Andreas Hilbeck / pixelio.de

More available books at **www.hansebooks.com**

# CONTENTS.

### CHAPTER I.

Incidents on the way—In London—On the Steamship "Kinsembo"—Monsieur de Haut—Gunpowder and candles—Bay of Biscay—Human fishes—Funchal—Musings—Land on the port bow—Tall hats—What's in a name—What makes it bite?—Bonny—Ju-ju house The tom-tom—Burial at sea—Where are their spirits gone? . . . . . . . . . . . . . . . 7

### CHAPTER II.

Banana—Door of the Dark Continent—Confusion of tongues—Sabbath breaking—At half mast, . . . . 25

### CHAPTER III.

Steamship "Heron"—Change of diet—Mukimvika—Ponta da Lenha—Fetich rock—Boma—Jocko—Tundua, 32

### CHAPTER IV.

Matadi—The Hill Difficulty—Underhill Station—On the march—Traders and drink—Palabala, . . . . . . 41

## CHAPTER V.

Superstition — Very inattentive — Nganga — Idols and charms—Bullet proof—Stone of the earth—Nkasa, . 51

## CHAPTER VI.

Kanga Mpaka—Ornaments on the graves—Embalming his body—"Holely" ornaments—Is it wrong to steal?—Can he see spirits? . . . . . . . . . . . . . 62

## CHAPTER VII.

Jiggers — Steamship "Corisco" — Taking medicine — Sound of the drum—The orchestra—The nganga says it may, . . . . . . . . . . . . . . . . . 70

## CHAPTER VIII.

In camp—Chop-boxes—Rousing the camp—Bad people—Conquered but not subdued—The Luvu—Banza Manteke—Little Johnny—Under a vow—Smoking the body—The Nkimba—The sacred grove—Intruding—Ndoki, . . . . . . . . . . . . . . . . 79

## CHAPTER IX.

A great change—Church bells—Opposition—Never returned—Willing to suffer—I go back—Climbing the palm tree. . . . . . . . . . . . . . . . . 94

## CHAPTER X.

The Lunionzo—Baka mbizi—Stop that noise—Shade and shelter—Peace and sleep—He stepped upon a sharp rock—House of the stranger, . . . . . . . . . 103

## CHAPTER XI.

Mukumbungu—Seeking the unseen—My first fever—Nkebeni—Waiting at the table—Easily remembered—Deserted—Selfishness, . . . . . . . . . . . 112

## CHAPTER XII.

Hunting—Zinzou zazingi—Face to face—Still in death—A delicate morsel, . . . . . . . . . . . . 122

## CHAPTER XIII.

Lukungu—Elephants and crocodiles—The swing bridge—Lost his balance—Gymnast, . . . . . . . . . . 128

## CHAPTER XIV.

Paying the carriers—Difficult to satisfy—Rejoicing in his riches—Conquered at last, . . . . . . . . . . 133

## CHAPTER XV.

Mavuzi's letter—Kivuila's letter—Markets in Congo—In the market—The site of the market—Things for sale—Tempting morsels—Theft in the market—Awful punishment, . . . . . . . . . . . . . . . . 140

## CHAPTER XVI.

Stanley Pool—The Bateke—Leopoldville—Upper Congo traders—On board the "Henry Reed"—The beauties of the Pool—No ketch bottom—A frog concert—The "En Avant"—Extended jaws—A narrow escape—Clock Point—Seized by a crocodile—U-p-r-a-a—Bolobo—Bolobo natives—Let go that fish—Malamu baa—Mode of execution—A weird scene—Nyama baa—Wa-t-ch—Collars not of linen—Killed by a buffalo, . 150

## CHAPTER XVII.

Equator Station—Buy me, Ingileza—Curious questions—Are they making soup?—Oh, thy pocket is empty—A visit from savages—Shut your eyes, . . . . . 175

## CHAPTER XVIII.

Woman stealers—Wadz'okum—Who is the greatest?—Longest arms—Kilolo hymn—Closing article—Light for Ethiopia, . . . . . . . . . . . . . 185

# LIFE AND SCENES IN CONGO.

## CHAPTER I.

INCIDENTS ON THE WAY—IN LONDON—ON THE STEAMSHIP KIN-
SEMBO—MONSIEUR DE HAUT—GUNPOWDER AND CANDLES—BAY
OF BISCAY—HUMAN FISHES—FUNCHAL—MUSINGS—LAND ON THE
PORT BOW—TALL HATS—WHAT'S IN A NAME—WHAT MAKES IT
BITE—BONNY—JU-JU HOUSE—THE TOM-TOM—BURIAL AT SEA—
WHERE ARE THEIR SPIRITS GONE?

FOG and smoke effectually obscured the blue sky as, for the fifth time, I found myself in the world's metropolis, the city of London. Our train, on the Great Western Railway, rolled into Paddington Station as evening shadows fell. After a short ride on the Metropolitan Underground Railroad, I emerged into daylight, or rather gaslight, at Aldgate Street Station. Here we were speedily hailed with "Cab, sir?" "'ansom, sir?" "Four wheeler?" But though heavily burdened, we could not afford a cab or 'ansom, even minus the letter "H," so we moved off in the direction of a friendly horse car which was en route for the East End. The especial object of our visit to the city was to make a few purchases in the shape of an outfit—light clothing, white umbrella, pith helmet, traveling bed and blankets, bath, medicines, carpenters' tools, cooking utensils such as saucepan, frying pan, enameled plates, cups and saucers, knives, forks, and spoons, traveling chair, small tent, etc. It took several days to secure the aforementioned articles, especially the etcs. Of this little outfit, some things are in Central Africa; some are at the bottom of the Congo; while others are at the bottom of the Atlantic Ocean. While in London, I was hospitably entertained at Harley College. Although Mr. H. Grattan Guinness was absent, yet I found a little chamber, and a bed, and a table, and a stool, and a candlestick, for the man of God.

Having completed my purchases, and arrangements for the voyage, and having again visited relatives and friends, Tuesday morning found me at the offices of Elder, Dempsey & Co., of Liverpool. After taking in the many sights of this great seaport, on Wednesday morning we went on board our steamer, the "Kinsembo" of the African Steam Navigation Com-

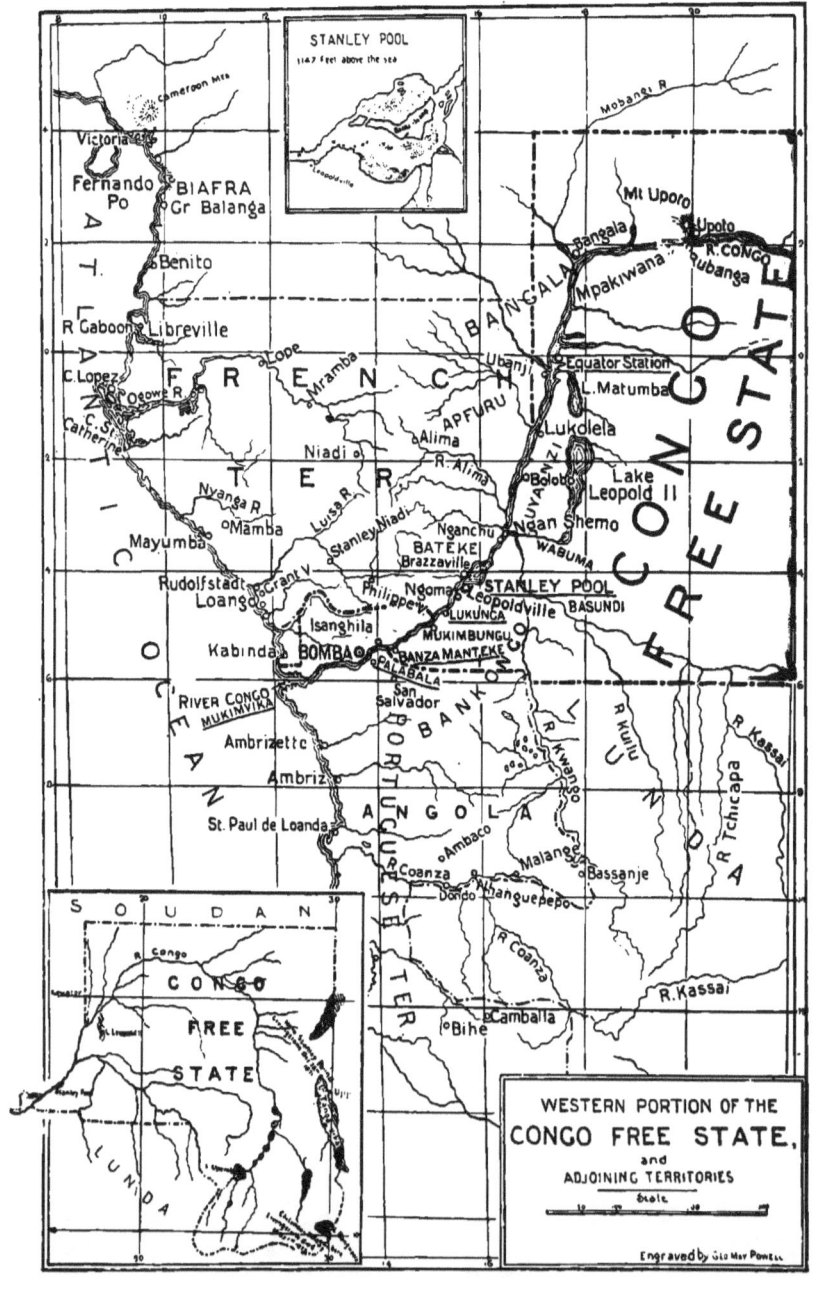

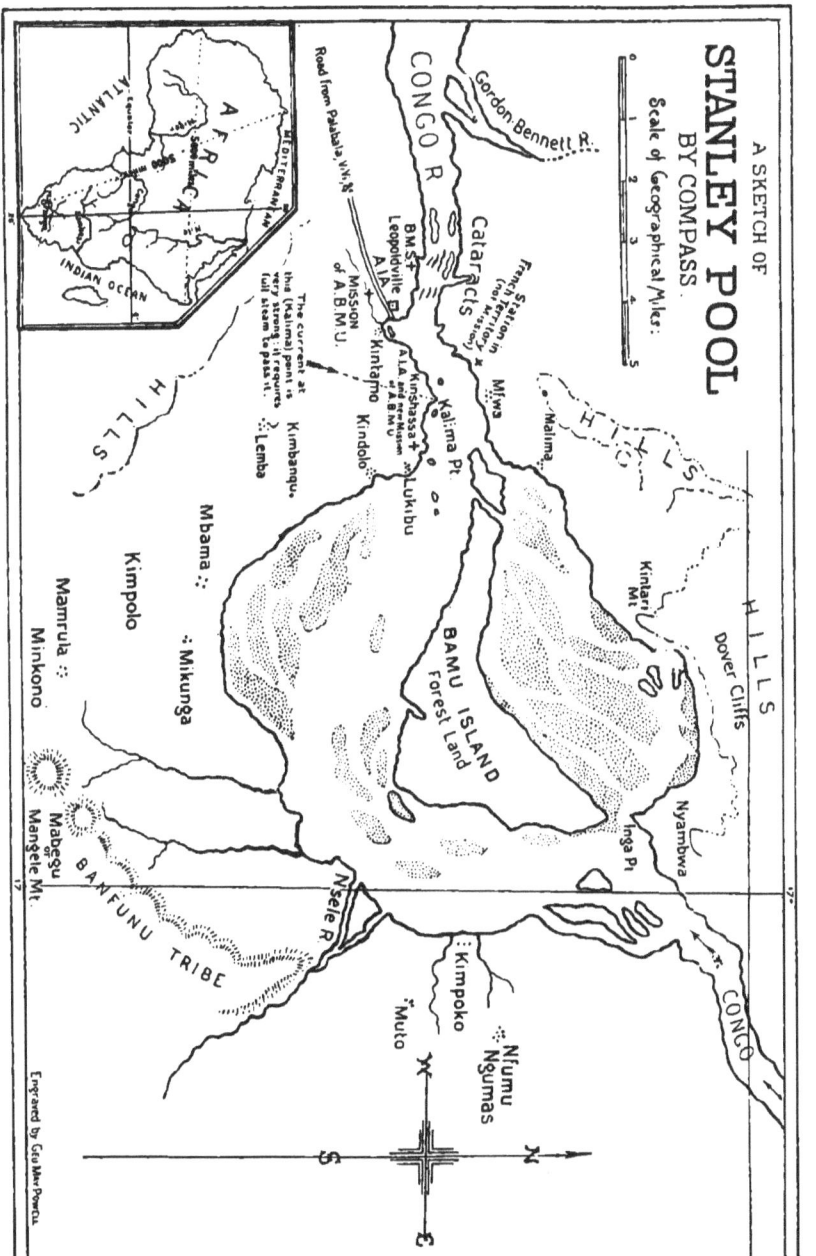

pany. What a crowd there was on the tender! I thought we were to have a large number of passengers. There were not many Christians in the crowd, for clinking glasses and drinking healths seemed the order of the day. Down in our little state room, just before the tender left, I, an ex-missionary, together with my dear brother and his wife, spent a brief season in prayer.

Presently the bell rang, and the usual "All ashore" from stentorian lungs was heard. Most of the supposed passengers went over the gangway to the tender, until there were but four of us on the "Kinsembo." Immediately the plank was withdrawn and we were under weigh. As we steamed down the Mersey, and as the tender returned to the landing stage, I gazed upon my dear brother and sister, and Picton, as long as I could distinguish them. To them *I* was the object of interest. As my brother afterward wrote: "It was not the old vessel that I cared so much about, but a portion of her cargo." As I have intimated, we were but four passengers, so it did not take us long to introduce ourselves to each other. There was myself, first American Baptist Missionary to Congo.

Passenger number two was a smart young Scotchman, Mr. Jaynes, whose parents were members of the Baptist Church, Hereford, England. Passenger number three was a colored man, and a native of Gaboon, which is a French possession. He claimed to be a son of the late king of Gaboon, and when asked his name, promptly gave it as Prince Makaga Ndinga. He was a man of Cetewayo's build, spoke English and French fairly well, and was an interesting companion. The fourth passenger was a French gentleman, Monsieur de Haut, bound for Libreville, Gaboon. He was a chemist, a lover of natural history, and fond of hunting. Whenever we passed a school of porpoises, he fired excitedly, frequently missing, but sometimes wounding the harmless, playful creatures. When, in the Calabar River, he fired at a shark, I was pleased; when he tried to hit a crocodile, I was glad; but why kill or wound the porpoise? Whenever we passed them, they gave us a free entertainment, disporting themselves around our steamer, and leaped, or swam, or dived, as though for our especial amusement.

One evening we found the monsieur in the saloon,

busily engaged, in order to pass the time, in recharging cartridges. On the table before him was a heap of powder, together with caps, bullets, empty cartridges, and a lighted candle. As we had paid for our passage to the mouth of the Congo, and having regard to our own welfare, we quietly called the attention of the Italian steward to the situation. At the same moment the purser came in and there was quite a little breeze. The purser promptly "put out the light," as he felt that it and the powder were in unpleasant proximity to each other. So, while our friend got a blowing up, we were not blown up.

We had a fifth passenger, for, last but not least, there was the monsieur's dog, a huge mastiff. So my readers will see that there was a small but select party on board the steamship "Kinsembo," as on June 17th, 1885, she steamed down the Mersey into the Irish Sea.

When we crossed the Bay of Biscay, I will not say that the sea rolled mountains high. As a matter of fact, it never rolls mountains high, but it was rough. My bosom heaved with the motion (emotion) of the steamer, and I paid tribute, again and again, to Father Neptune. This seemed singular, as I had before this sailed over many thousands of miles of deep blue sea. On the second day, my stomach performed its office without a murmur, my feet and ankle bones recovered strength, and I stood upon my sea legs. The "Kinsembo" did not go directly to Congo. Our first stopping place was the sunny Isle of Madeira, with its harbor of Funchal, whose waters are so very clear. I wish my readers could see the little Portuguese boys, in their boats around our steamer, and hear them shout, "Senor, throw sixpence in water." "Bring it up in my teeth." "Pick it up between my toes." "Throw far way." "Dive under steamer for six pence, senor." A German gentleman who came on board threw money several times. He had just returned from his ostrich farm in South Africa, so he had a deeper purse than I, or than even Prince Makaga. We could see the bright silver sinking into the depths as a boy dived after it. Each time he appeared with the coin in his teeth or between his toes. For a sixpence, another boy dived right under our steamer, a depth of over twenty-five feet. There was no danger here from sharks, but diving so frequently must surely be very injurious. Dear little fellows! why were they not in school ? Alas ! schools here are few and far between ; and such schools ! In this beautiful isle of the sea everything is controlled by Romanists. A number of men came on board with articles for sale. Among these were fancy needlework, ornamental writing desks and work baskets ; rattan and wicker work of all descriptions, such as chairs, sofas, tables, etc. Some offered for sale photographs of the town of Funchal, while others had birds of every hue and plumage, inviting the inspection of the traveler. I did not make a purchase, as I was going the wrong way. The surf was bad, but I made a hurried visit to the town, put my letters in the " correio " or post office, and accompanied by Mr. Jaynes and Prince Makaga, I went into the large Roman Catholic church. It was a high day, and though the hour was early, the church was well filled. All were evidently in earnest. We looked upon them as they came out. Why those dissatisfied, gloomy countenances ? Out upon such a religion, that cannot give joy to the heart nor peace to the soul.

Leaving the sunny isle, the "Kinsembo" was steered for the west coast of Africa. I may be pardoned for introducing here these few lines, written soon after leaving Madeira. They were spontaneous and very imperfect, but here they are:

>  'Tis night,
> The stars are shrouded in a veil of mist;
> The sickly moon through hazy clouds is faintly shining.
> In Southern waters sailing—off Madeira's Isle,
> I pace the quarter-deck alone, alone,
> Then cease my step to muse awhile;
> To think of you, and "home, sweet home."
> Home, where my aged sire, whose once athletic form
> Is bending now toward the tomb; and that dear one who
>     gave me birth,
> With wrinkled brow and whitened locks,
> Like ripened grain, fit for the sickle,
> Sit round the evening fire, and fondly talk
> About their absent boy.
> Methinks I hear the echo of their prayer:
> "Father of love and power;
> Hear thou us in this hour;
> Thy richest blessings pour
>     Upon our absent boy.
> Keep him in Congo land,
> And may he firmly stand,
> One of thy faithful band,
>     True to his God."

When about four hundred miles south of Madeira, we sighted Teneriffe's "cloud-piercing height." We passed close to the island. The base of the mount was wrapped in cold, gray clouds, but thirteen thousand feet above it pierced the clouds, and its summit was bathed in sunlight. We thought of Goldsmith's lines, in his description of a good man:

> "Though round its breast the rolling clouds are spread,
> Eternal sunshine settles on its head."

Between Teneriffe and the west coast, and when out of sight of land, a pretty and gaudily-arrayed butterfly flew around the quarter-deck, as though it came to bid us welcome to tropical Africa. One morning a flying fish fell on board. It was soon in the scientific hands of Monsieur de Haut, who wanted the *poisson volant* (flying fish) to add to his collection of treasures.

Hurrah! Land on the port bow. Our first sight of Africa. Away in the distance, we could just descry the dim outline of the African coast. The experienced eye of the captain not only saw land, but recognized it as a part of the Kru coast. We drew near the shore, then hove to and fired a heavy gun. Through our glasses we could very plainly discern a commotion, and a rush for the steamer. In an hour the forward deck was crowded with Kru boys. Some came to work, and others came to trade and to take back the canoes. These stalwart fellows were naked, save a small cloth around the loins. I observed that the sailors in the forecastle were doing a roaring trade with the Kru boys. The Kru boys take a fancy to tall chimney-pot hats. The sailors had gotten an inkling of this on a previous voyage, and provided a large number, attractive in appearance, but very cheap. These the Kru men eagerly purchased with ivory, parrots, monkeys, skins, fish, and fruits. Soon they came marching majestically along the deck, crowned with a tall hat, which was still covered with the white paper. Those who purchased the tall hats were loth to return to their canoes.

Captain Jolly was impatient to get under weigh, and the visitors would not retire, so orders were given to start the engines full speed. Then there was a scene. The owners of the hats mounted the ship's sides, and plunged into the rough waters, completely submerging the tall hats. This afforded great delight to the other men on board. We were also amused, and I could hear the deep, gutteral laugh of Prince

Makaga, as he looked upon the men struggling to get to their canoes. With every group of Kru boys there is a headman or leader. He has charge of them, and each one pays him a small portion of his wages. These headmen have been down the coast before, and can jabber away in English, French, or Portuguese, to the extent of about twelve words. They are named by the officers of the ship or by traders. The headmen on our steamer rejoiced in the names of "*Pea-soup,*" "*Kettle-of-Fish,*" and "*Sea-breeze.*" Pea-soup was a fairly good fellow, had a great sense of humor, but, like many others, was sadly demoralized through drink. He was a tall man, and his legs turned in at the knees. The only article of clothing he wore was an old shirt, and he cut quite a figure as he moved around looking after his men. Pea-soup and Kettle-of-Fish were rather jealous of each other, and frequently had a great palaver. I must confess I regarded Pea-soup as the better man.

When in Liverpool I purchased a small galvanic battery, and this afforded the Kru boys much amusement. I placed one handle in a bowl of water on one of the hatches, and my German friend put a coin in the water. The Kru men looked on. After explaining matters a little, and stating conditions, I called for a volunteer, who was soon forthcoming. He seized one handle with a vise-like grip, and with the other hand attempted to take up the coveted coin. With an awful yell it was instantly withdrawn, and he started forward on a run. I shall not soon forget the expression of fear and surprise on their faces. Several tried, with the same result. The headman was instructed to ask: "White man, what make water bite?"

After calling at several places, we arrived at the Bight of Benin. Here many Kru men went on shore to work. There were three other steamers in the Bight, and of what do you think their cargo consisted? Cloth? No. Food? No. Missionaries to teach the heathen? No, alas, no. Mostly rum. For whom was the rum intended? For the poor, unenlightened African. Steamer after steamer comes down the coast, sometimes with a quantity of merchandise, or a few heralds of the cross, but for the most part laden with rum, and that, horrid stuff at best. Oh, America, your skirts are even now red with the blood of your victims! Spare the poor African! Give him a chance in the race of life!

Leaving Benin, we proceeded to Bonny, which is situated on one of the mouths of the Niger River, and is the home of King "Oko Jumbo." Myself, Mr. Jaynes, and the prince went through the native town, which lies so low that we found the effluvium from the rank and decaying vegetation very great. Among other places, we visited the Ju-ju house. I imagine my readers pause and ask, "What is a Ju-ju house?" It is a place where the people practice their superstitious rites. Inside the house was a heap of human bones, while the outside was decorated with the skulls of the many victims who had been slain in battle, or at their religious feasts. I inwardly loathed the sickening sight, and gladly turned away. Most of the children in this town were nearly naked; many quite so.

During our ramble, we paid a visit to Chief Alison, or, as he gave his name, "Jamaica Alison, Esq." As Jamaica Alison, Esq., walked along to his home, a slave walked behind him, holding a huge gaudy umbrella over the head of his chief.

Nearly all chiefs in Bonny keep slaves. We saw many large canoes on the river, manned by slaves, and on which the "tom-tom" seemed an indispensable piece of music. It is made by fixing pieces of different kinds of wood on strings across the canoe, and the musician sitting behind the chief, with two sticks, produces music something like "Rum-tum-tum, rum-tum-tum, rum-tum-tum-tum." The effect is all the better when heard at a distance.

After our return to the "Kinsembo," we had an introduction to another Bonny man, Warribo Merilla Pepple, commander-in-chief of the Bonny forces. He was a shrewd old gentleman.

While at Bonny, I spoke in the little Episcopal church, the first time I spoke on African soil.

From Bonny we went to Old Calabar. While I visited the Presbyterian Mission, Monsieur de Haut spent a whole day in hunting. He returned at night, tired, hungry, and thirsty, and with no game; not even the carcass of a monkey.

After calling at Fernando Po and San Tome, we anchored at Libreville, Gaboon, which is on the equator. Here Monsieur de Haut left us. We often thought of him. Does he yet live? Was he smitten by the African fever? Did he come to grief on some hazardous hunting expedition? Or is he now in some town or jungle in the interior, collecting specimens in the interests of science, or hunting, or making observations among the Sierra Complida? I do not know. Here, too, was the home of Makaga Ndinga. I went to the home of the prince, and found it a comfortable house. His wife came down to the beach to meet him, and chided him for staying away so long. Evidently she thought he had spent too much money; and he was certainly dressed more fashionably than his relatives. Poor Prince Makaga! his glory is departed. His princely rank is not recognized by the French, although, perhaps, more worthy of recognition than is that of some other princes we know.

From Gaboon we proceeded to Mayumba. Here Bishop Taylor, I was told, had planted a mission, which, it was hoped, would soon become self-supporting. The experience of the brethren as reported to me was far from satisfactory. As to the question of self-support in African missions—among native preachers we think it possible, but among white men we think it impracticable. It is a foreign land to the white man. His constitution cannot endure as much fatigue as in his own country. To the white man on the unhealthy west coast of Africa, "the time is short." It is short and very precious, and it does not pay for him to till the soil and erect his dwelings. He may, and should superintend all this, but he will find sufficient scope for the exercise of his physical powers in other directions.

Here at Mayumba, one of the pioneers of the English Baptist Mission to Congo was buried, on June 28, 1887. I refer to the Rev. T. J. Comber, who died the second day from Banana, while on his way home in the German steamship, "Lulu Bohlen." Among his last words were these:

> "O Christ, thou art the fountain,
> The deep spring-well of love;
> The springs of earth I've tasted——"

and almost with these words on his lips, he passed away to be with Christ, whom he so loved.

Our only other stopping place before we reached Congo was Kabenda. It is forty miles north of the

Congo. The "Kinsembo" stayed here two days, and so we went on shore. Some distance up from the beach, and near to several traders' establishments, there is a little "God's Acre." Here lies Rev. Henry Craven, formerly of Palabala, and one of the first missionaries from England to Congo. After six years of faithful service, he died in 1884. Feeling somewhat run down, he left Palabala, and came to Kabenda, to Mr. McCready, of the English factory. Here he was again stricken with his old trouble, from which he never rallied, but passed to that land where "neither shall the sun light on them, nor any heat." As I stood near the grave of the honored dead, methought I heard a voice exclaim, " Blessed are the dead which die in the Lord from henceforth ; yea, saith the spirit, that they may rest from their labors ; and their works do follow them." Here in his lonely grave sweetly he sleeps, while the restless waters of the Atlantic and the breezes among the graceful palm trees sing his requiem.

Between Mayumba and Kabenda two Kru boys died. Their bodies were speedily sewn up in canvas, and for the first time in my life I saw a burial at sea.

The bodies were placed upon one of the hatches, then with little ceremony, and without checking the speed of the steamer, they were consigned to the great deep. At the word of command, other Kru boys lifted the hatch; two plunges into the water, and all was over. How little did these poor Kru boys know of the world's Redeemer! The Atlantic took their bodies; whither went their spirits? Not to heaven, for, "there shall in no wise enter into it anything that defileth;" and while few of these men know of Christ, they sin, sometimes ignorantly; sometimes against light and knowledge. We never yet found any one who lived up to the light he possessed. We have no sympathy with the theory of a second probation. We believe that the eternal destiny of all men is unalterably fixed at death, to say the least of it. We do not think that the Africans are "sinners above all sinners;" others perhaps sin far more than they. God will judge them righteously. "As many as have sinned *without* law, shall also *perish* without law; and as many as have sinned *in* the law, shall be judged *by* the law."

## CHAPTER II.

BANANA—DOOR OF THE DARK CONTINENT—CONFUSION OF
TONGUES—SABBATH BREAKING—AT HALF-MAST.

LEAVING Kabenda at eight in the morning, we made our last run, arriving at Banana, on the Congo, at four in the afternoon. The whole sea, long before we came near Banana, at the entrance of the Congo River, was of a deep brown color, and of quite fresh water, with a strong current running toward the ocean. The mouth of the Congo is very deep. Recent soundings have established the fact that the main channel at the mouth of river is over fourteen hundred feet deep, or more than a quarter of a mile. The width of the river at the mouth is seven and a half miles. Farther inland, where it passes through narrow gorges, or branches out into creeks, where the land lies low, its width is from one to fifteen miles. The actual source of the Congo is still a matter of conjecture, and hence its length cannot yet be fully determined. If it rises in the Urungu Mountains, flows through Lakes Bangueolo and Moero, then its length must be three thousand miles. It receives into its bosom the waters of many mighty rivers, as the Lomami, the Arawimi, the Itembiri, the Lolongo, the Juapa, the Mobangi, the Kua, the Kasai and the Sankuru; also smaller rivers, such as Ikilemba, the Kimpoko, the Gordon-Bennett, the Luila, the Nkalama, the Lulovo, the Nkisi, the Lunzadi, the Manene, the Luasa, the Mpioka, the Luwa, the Lukunga, the Kuilu, the Lunionso, the Luvu, the Bembizi, the Nduzi, and the Mpozo, and many others; with a large number of somewhat smaller streams. Banana, which is situated on a promontory at the mouth of the river, is a place of considerable importance, as the headquarters of many trading companies. The languages of nearly all civilized nations may be heard here. To this may be added the mysterious nasal jargon of many natives from all parts of the west coast. The Dutch have a large factory here, employing thirty to forty white men, and several hundred natives. There are also Portuguese, Spanish, French, German, and English houses, all of which employ a goodly number of men. A difference of opinion exists as to the healthfulness of Banana, compared with other parts of the Congo. Some consider that there is more malaria there than farther up the river. Others declare that they enjoy fairly good health there. Statistics as to the mortality of white men at Banana are unsatisfactory, many having died from preventable causes. In 1882 one missionary died at Banana, Mr. W. Appel. He sailed in May, arrived in June, and died in July. At the time it was believed that his death was due to over exertion. How far that is correct, I cannot say. Some white traders have lived there for eight, ten, and twelve years at one time. Mr. Phillips, of the English house, has lived there for ten years without intermission. Banana is not a town, as there are no streets. It is simply made up of trading houses, and the promontory upon which it is situated is narrow and largely artificial. On one side is the Atlantic Ocean, and on the other is a large creek, which empties into the Congo. I have been puzzled to know why it was called Banana, for there are no bananas growing anywhere near.

When I arrived I was unexpectedly met by representatives from the Dutch house, and by a brother missionary. I was glad and sorry to leave the "Kinsembo." Glad, because I had reached Banana. Sorry, because, having been on board forty-three days, I had a feeling of attachment for the steamer and for the officers. The officials of the Dutch house were very kind to us, and placed a room, such as it was, at our disposal. At seven in the evening I sat down with about thirty white men to a meal called in Portuguese, "jantar," or dinner. It was served in a large room, which was open on three sides, thus affording a refreshing breeze from the Atlantic. Other meals are served at 7 A. M., "café;" and at 11 A. M., "almoço," or breakfast. I was tired, and glad to get to bed at nine, and spend my first night in Africa, during which mosquitoes and fleas gave me a warm reception. In the morning I discovered that a dishonest rat had actually attempted to carry off one of my boots. Failing in that, he ate the tongue of one. I found the boot across the rat hole in a corner of my room. What a thief! The next morning found me again on board the "Kinsembo," trying to get my few boxes and bales on shore. This was by no means an easy task, but by a little planning and coaxing we managed it. My brother missionary, Mr. Banks, brought our boat, "The Moffat," from Mukimvika, with a crew of natives, to ply the oars and to handle my stuff. What a jolly fellow Banks was! How the natives enjoyed his society! These Mukimvika men, like all Congo natives, have a great sense of humor. Any joke or funny remark that comes within the range of their ideas is irresistible. They are not dull of comprehension and can readily see a point. I found the gentlemen at the Dutch house very courteous and hospitable. At the table there was a perfect Babel of tongues, thoughts being exchanged in English, French, Dutch, Portuguese and Ki-kongo. Each white man keeps a boy to wait upon him at the table, and these little fellows have usually a smattering of one or two languages besides their own. I discovered, however, that few of the boys understood English. Happily, I had prepared a very limited vocabulary of Portuguese and Ki-kongo. I thought it sounded so queer for me, a Welsh-English-American, to ask in Portuguese, "Da me agua" (give me water); or "Nzolele nlangu" (I want water) in Ki-kongo.

In the tropics, the days being short, supper is eaten by lamp light. After spending one or more nights in the guests' room, rather exposed to the vicious attacks of mosquitoes, I awoke with a fearful headache, and a feverish pulse. It was Sunday morning, bright and beautiful. At Banana, there is little labor performed on the Lord's Day; the white men visit each other, while the natives rest and lounge about. Though it is the Lord's Day, it is not observed as such, for there is probably more sin committed on that day than on any other. Banana is about equally divided between Satan and Jesuit priests. A hotel has recently been built by the Dutch Trading Company, which is situated right on the promontory, and is a most convenient stopping place for Congo travelers while waiting for the up river or ocean steamers. The charges are high—about three dollars and fifty cents per day—but the food and accommodation are good. When I sojourned there, the chief was a Spaniard; the sub-chief was a Portuguese, while Loango boys acted as cooks and waiters.

As may be expected, spirituous liquors are sold in this hotel, and there is also a billiard table. Here, on Sunday afternoons, white men of all nationalities almost, meet to drink, to play billiards, or to dance. Thus they keep the Lord's Day, and the colored employés are at the same hour enjoying themselves on the sea beach, in the surf, or beneath the shade of palm trees in the grove, drinking fermented palm wine, or something stronger, and more destructive. It is extremely difficult to get a substantial hold of these poor natives, because of contact with the grossest elements of civilization. Deaths are frequent among them, but still they pursue their course of sin.

One can not but have a feeling of sympathy for the traders here and elsewhere on the African rivers, who are so isolated and cut off from all good influences. Our conversation with at least one trader at Banana was most interesting. Do they in the midst of their hilarity, or in moments of reflection, ever think of death, of God, or judgment, or eternity? Let us hope some do. More than once during our visits to the coast, we have seen the flags at the various establishments, flying at half mast—another death; another soul gone from the Banana trading houses, to give an account of the deeds done in the body.

# CHAPTER III.

STEAMSHIP HERON—CHANGE OF DIET—MUKIMVIKA—PONTA DA LENHA—FETICH ROCK—BOMA—JOCKO—TUNDUA.

EARLY on Sunday morning it was reported that the steamship "Heron" would shortly leave for up the river. Mr. Banks and I proceeded to make inquiries. At the offices of the Congo Free State we met an official of whom we asked:

"Does the 'Heron' leave to-day?"

"She will leave this morning."

"How far will she go?"

"To Matadi."

This place was one hundred and ten miles from the coast, and ten miles from Palabala, our objective point.

"Can you favor us with passage?"

"Well, we will try and accommodate you, gentlemen."

"Many thanks. Our boys will at once get our blankets and a few other things."

Our time was limited, so we made haste to secure a few articles, leaving most of our baggage behind. We did not forget to provide a little for the wants of the body. I obtained one dozen oranges while at Kabenda, while Mr. Banks opened a case of provisions and took a tin of biscuits.

With the oranges and biscuits and a little of the Congo water, we felt we would not suffer seriously for a day or two. This was a rather severe change to me, having fared so well on board the "Kinsembo." However, it prepared me in a measure for other and more severe experiences.

The "Heron" was a small river steamer, with light draught. In order to give meagre accommodations to each, we were stowed away very snugly on the small deck around the wheel, while an awning of woodwork protected us from the pitiless rays of a burning sun. A Scotchman was at the engines and a native at the wheel. The man at the wheel, not being quite familiar with the duties of a helmsman and pilot, needed the constant attention of the captain, who supplemented his instructions and warnings with frequent blows.

At 10 A. M. we steamed out of Banana creek and steered right for Bulambemba Point. Navigation is difficult on many parts of the river, owing to the strong currents and whirlpools that have to be avoided. We soon sighted Mukimvika Station. This Mission Station of the American Baptist Missionary Union, "beautiful for situation," is on rising ground, but ten minutes walk from the nearest part of the river, and about fifteen miles from Banana. One of the chiefs here is known as King Plenty. The surroundings of this station are almost like an English park. It is in Portuguese territory. A great part of the land near Mukimvika is intersected by creeks, some of them so narrow and winding, and almost covered by the overhanging vegetation, that boats must be carefully steered. This is the home of the mangrove tree. When the tide ebbs, the black muddy roots of the mangroves are exposed to view, thereby diffusing an odor none of the pleasantest or most healthful. Mukimvika is a noted place for parrots. The natives are very expert in climbing trees and catching the young birds. These they take to Banana and sell to traders and travelers. They usually cost

Life and Scenes in Congo.        Page 31.
A MANGROVE.

about one dollar and a quarter each, and more if it can be gotten. The money thus obtained is converted into necklaces or other ornaments, but is rarely used as a currency. The natives prefer English money to French or Portuguese.

Elephants' tails were formerly in great demand in this district—*i. e.*, the hairs or bristles that form the end of the tail. One or more of them hung around the neck was believed to act as a charm, and is regarded as a thing of beauty. Some years ago, a fowl could be purchased for one of these hairs. The creeks near Mukimvika are infested with crocodiles, and it is unsafe to bathe. One little boy who was in our mission went with others down to the creek, probably to swim, for the children are so fearless. In this creek were many large crocodiles, or, as a native would say, "Zingandu zazinene zazingi." The boy was seized by one of these reptiles, and never afterward seen.

Passing Mukimvika, we soon sighted Bull Island and Kisanga and Scotchman Head, where the river takes a sharp turn to the east. The scenery along the banks is worthy of all admiration, and I would that my readers could take just one glance at the Congo by Kisanga. The graceful palms overhanging the water; the dense jungles of mangroves, with their many huge roots visible several feet above the earth; the huge baobab with its unsightly and uneven trunk; the tree ferns, and the numerous delicate creepers, crowned by the creeping palm, with its bunches of beautiful scarlet dates—all tell of the rich tropical vegetation.

After steering past numerous low sandy islands, we made for Ponta Da Lenha, which is about twenty-five miles from Banana. Here there is an English trading house, as also those of the Dutch and French. These houses are almost enclosed by tall trees and impenetrable tropical vegetation. The whole neighborhood consists of endless winding creeks, bamboo swamps, and dense forests. Leaving Ponta Da Lenha, we continued our voyage. At 4 P. M. we passed Fetich Rock, a point of interest to all travelers up the Congo. It is a high ledge of rocks jutting far out into the river on the south bank. The river at this point is deep and the current swift, and years ago lives were sacrificed at this rock. Natives assembled in great numbers from the surrounding districts, and after going through painful and foolish ceremonies, the poor victims were thrown from the rock into the Congo, thus terminating their sufferings. Many of these were half dead before their awful plunge into the river, while crocodiles were invariably near enough to seize them as they fell. The presence of traders in the neighborhood, and the frequent passing of steamers up and down the river, has contributed to the discontinuance of this most inhuman practice.

In 1885, the steamship "Ville du Antwerp" was lost at Fetich Rock. If I remember rightly, Sir Francis de Winton and one or two other white men, together with a number of natives, were on board. While passing this point, the ship struck a hidden rock, and went down very quickly. The white men and a few of the natives were saved, but several Kru boys were drowned.

It was 6.45 P. M., when our little steamer, the "Heron," drew up alongside the landing stage at Boma. Here we engaged several natives to carry our stuff to the Dutch house, where we were to spend the night. It was now quite dark. The day had been long and warm, and even our biscuits and oranges did not seem to afford complete satisfaction, for we reached Boma tired and hungry. Boma has a number of traders' establishments, and almost every nation is represented here as well as at Banana. Boma is also the headquarters of the Congo Free State. This gives to this otherwise insignificant place an air of official importance. There is a sanatarium here for the benefit of the Congo Free State officials, and it is the official residence of the governor of the Congo. This office was first filled by Mr. H. M. Stanley, then by Sir Francis de Winton. Latterly, King Leopold of Belgium has conferred the governorship upon Belgian officers.

Mr. Caseman, one of the Free State officials, came with us from Banana, who had with him a large specimen of the chimpanzee, which was captured on the West coast of Africa. As I looked at him quietly munching some food, I thought I would not like to engage in an encounter with a full-grown specimen, in the forests of his native home. On the banks of the Congo, and in the forest, I frequently saw many small specimens of the monkey tribe. At least one gorilla has been captured on the Congo. These are more dangerous than the chimpanzee, but happily they are very seldom seen, as one would not care to make their personal acquaintance, unless they were behind the bars of a cage.

At eight o'clock in the morning we again embarked, and this time were joined by a French Jesuit priest from Boma, where there is a Jesuit mission. On our way to Matadi, we passed various trading posts, Noki, Masuka, etc. Near to Matadi the river makes another sharp turn to the east, and navigation is very difficult at this point. No one who has ever passed Tundua will forget the seething, boiling, rushing water, pushing its way to the sea with irresistible force, while on either side the hills rise to a height of several hundred feet. The depth of the river around the bend is nine hundred feet, and steamers are compelled to put on high pressure in order to struggle through these strong waters. Even then they have frequently to back down and try again. In 1885, a large man-of-war steamer came up past Tundua as far as Vivi, several miles beyond. In rounding the point she nearly went over on her beam ends. The commander and others on board were greatly alarmed, but after considerable manœuvering she got past the point of strongest resistance.

The steamship "Heron" went through it right nobly, though, at one time, it seemed as if we could never push through the strong current. The little engine, like a thing of life, exerted itself to its utmost, making the waters hiss and seethe, and raising a perfect whirlpool astern, and in half an hour we were past Tundua Point.

# CHAPTER IV.

MATADI—THE HILL DIFFICULTY—UNDERHILL STATION—ON THE
MARCH—TRADERS AND DRINK—PALABALA.

JUST before we arrived at Tundua Point, we sighted a boat, with a white man in it.

"Hallo," said Banks, "there's the E. B. M. boat"; which means the English Baptist Mission boat. We were anxious to get a boat to bring us from Matadi to the English Baptist Mission House, where we were to spend the night. The mission house is situated on the summit of the Tundua hill, and commands a magnificent view of the river.

The Rev. Mr. Moolenar and several natives were in the boat, and our signal was seen and replied to.

Soon after our arrival at Matadi, the priest departed down river in a canoe, while Mr. Banks and myself were cared for by Mr. Moolenar. In passing the point once more, we kept close to the shore to avoid the strong water. Of course, we were objects of interest to the Loanga boys who handled the oars. Might not the white men bless them with a "dash" of cloth, or something in the shape of food? There is a path leading right from the water up to the mission; so, immediately after disembarking, we commenced the trying ascent.

Happily, the sun was sinking into the western sky, so that its burning rays no longer poured down upon us, and the Loango boys did us good service by carrying our few things up the ascent. We found locomotion very trying, however, without the addition of a load. As we struggled upward, I thought of Beattie's lines:

"Ah, who can tell, how hard it is to climb
The steep, where Fame's proud temple shines afar."

I thought of Bunyan's "Hill Difficulty"; I thought of Longfellow's "Excelsior." Our objective point, however, was not a temple of fame, but a mission house. The location of this English Baptist Mission is a fine one, affording a splendid view up and down the river for many miles. When representatives of the Baptist Missionary Society first established themselves, they built at the *foot* of the hill, since it was more convenient to the river. Afterward, a new house complete was sent out from England and erected near the summit. It is called Underhill Station, not because it was originally at the foot of the hill, but in honor of Dr. Underhill of London.

This mission house is the most substantial and comfortable of any in Congo. It is built on pillars on account of the white ants, and a good veranda all round affords a grateful shade. It is reached from the garden path by broad iron steps. The garden is well laid out. Paw-paw, lime, and orange trees are planted there, and it also furnishes a goodly supply of vegetables.

Not far from the station there is a little plot of land fenced in as a cemetery, in which lie the remains of several young missionaries. Some of these were called to a higher service before they even commenced active service in the land of their adoption. In each case, I believe, fever was the immediate cause of death. They left England, fitted, as they thought, for a term of service for the Master in Congo-land. "Yet their pilgrimage was shorter, and their trials sooner done." The brethren at this mission, Moolenar and Charters, gave us a very kindly welcome.

In the morning Mr. Banks and I prepared to depart, but both of our brethren had contracted fever, and were unable to rise, so Banks and I got things in readiness for the march to Palabala, a distance of eight to ten miles.

At 7.30 we were ready for the road, and a sorry road it proved to be. The "njila" (road) in Congo is but a narrow pathway, affording sufficient room for one person only; two can seldom travel abreast. I was properly equipped for traveling; my trousers were light, and my stockings were drawn up over them. I wore no vest, and no coat. A pith helmet, and white umbrella with green lining protected me from the sun, while each of us carried a long bamboo stick to assist us in climbing the hills. Our Loango boys were in good spirits; the march was to be a short one—at Palabala they expected to receive their reward, or "dash."

Mr. Banks was a powerful man, and stepped out in fine style. Some carriers were in front and some behind, but all were marching single file. Seeing it was my first marching experience in Africa, we perhaps walked faster than we should have done under such a sun. However, I kept in Mr. Bank's tracks all the way, and could have taken the lead at any time. In about an hour and a half we began to descend a precipitous, rocky hill, at the foot of which is the valley along which flows the "Nzadi a Mpoza," or river of shade. This is a little more than half way from Underhill to Palabala, and is moderately deep and swift, the services of a ferryman being constantly necessary. A large number of caravans from up country cross the river Mpozo at this point, and Chief Kangampaka, of Palabala, derived a good revenue from the toll exacted from travelers and caravans. The canoes belonged to Kangampaka, while the ferryman was either a slave of the old chief, or one of his subjects. In either case, he was compelled to work for very small pay. From the Mpozo, roads lead in various directions to trading houses on the Congo. Some of the unprincipled traders have discovered that it pays to plant men who are well supplied with bottles of horrid stuff called rum, or gin, right at the Mpozo, to meet caravans coming down country, and, if possible, to intercept them. With this rum they can decoy the guileless native, and lead him and his ivory to their master's establishment.

As we approached the river, through the tall grass, our men, with their sharp eyes, discovered that the canoe was on the other side. The ferryman was some distance away in his little hut, enjoying himself; so our men, to save time, began shouting: "E tuala e nlungu e.—Tu zolele viokele nsualu ē." Translated into the language of English-speaking boys and girls, that would be, "Bring the canoe; we want to cross in haste."

Presently their shouts received a reply from the ferryman, who appeared through the doorless hut, and made for his canoe, or "nlungu."

"Nkwizanga kwami" (I am coming).

The canoe was speedily transferred to our side of the river, and Mr. Banks and myself stepped into it.

This canoe was simply a tree hollowed out by chipping and burning, and the trunk from which it was made was not quite straight. These canoes have to be evenly balanced, and are by no means safe. The natives are so familiar with water, and with their canoes, that they scarcely know what fear means;

besides, they swim like fishes, so that the only danger to them from an upturned canoe would be "zingandu," or crocodiles.

When we were properly stowed away in the canoe, our ferryman began to pull up the stream for some distance; then, with the prow of the canoe still pointing up stream, he began to pull across. Crocodiles are found up and down this river, and this did not increase our complacency.

Palabala is situated on a fine plateau, fully sixteen hundred feet above sea level. It is about one hundred and twenty miles from the mouth of the Congo, and ten miles from the south bank. Some of my readers doubtless know that there is a large cataract some few miles above Matadi—the Yelala Falls; and hence the lower river is navigable only to this point. Yelala Falls is the first of a series of cataracts and rapids, extending inland for a distance of two hundred and thirty miles, or as far as Leopoldville or Stanley Pool. Portions of the river between these cataracts and rapids are navigable, but, on the whole, the river between Matadi and Leopoldville is unsafe.

In a few minutes Banks and I reached the Palabala side of the Mpozo river, and immediately prepared ourselves for another stiff climb up the Palabala plateau. The sun was becoming warm, but we were in good spirits, and with our thin walking boots, stepped nimbly along. Here, let me say, Stanley advises all travelers in the tropics to wear moderately heavy laced boots, with thick soles. My experience taught me somewhat to the contrary. I found a light cricket boot with canvas uppers far more comfortable and less wearisome than a heavy laced leather boot.

In addition to the regular toll exacted by Kangampaka, our ferryman received a small " dash " for his ready service. As we moved from the river, our friend shouted : " Wenda kabiza." To which we replied : " Sala kabiza."

These are Congo expressions used at parting, and are about equivalent to: "Go in good condition ;" " Stay in good condition."

There are at least two roads leading from the Mpozo ferry to Palabala. The one passes through a town of considerable size, while the other avoids the towns and most of the native houses, and winds through a more sequestered district. On the former road, the ascent to the Palabala plateau is more gradual than along the other, and it is also longer and more circuitous. We chose the shorter path. Some parts of this road are fairly good, but it is severe climbing for the most part, and huge rocks and boulders lie in the path. We tried to avoid the sharp, jagged edges of the one and the smooth, slippery surface of the other.

Mr. Banks and I were trudging along right on the heels of our carriers, and we frequently shouted to them: "O zingambu, diata nsualu, nsualu" (O workman, walk quickly, quickly).

This would tickle them immensely, for they probably thought that they were stepping along nimbly enough, and indeed they were. They seemed, however, to conjecture that we wanted to reach our destination as soon as possible.

"Oh, the white man has come away from 'Ku'-mputu,' and he wants to see his friends at Palabala. Let us quickly walk, that he may get there before the sun will be right over us. He will then rejoice, and we may get small dash."

In some such talk they beguiled the monotony of

the short march. "Ku'mputu" means the foreign land. And "dash" means a present, and is commonly used all along the west coast.

When half way to Palabala, on the hillside, Mr. Banks suggested a temporary halt, and I willingly consented. Both of us were parched with thirst, but for a time, could not find a drop of water to remove that thirst. A few of my oranges yet remained, and never did oranges taste so sweet as those we ate on the Palabala hillside, under the imperfect shade of a small scrubby tree. After some searching, we did discover water, in a torrent bed or summer stream. It was a small pool not yet dried up, rank with vegetable matter, and well warmed by the sun. Ordinarily, my stomach would reject such vile stuff, but now my thirst was severe. The sight of such a pool as this would rejoice the heart of many a traveler in the deserts of Africa.

We sipped cautiously and sparingly, as no one could tell how much insect life was in each drop. All stagnant water in the tropics must teem therewith.

# CHAPTER V.

SUPERSTITION — VERY INATTENTIVE — NGANGA — IDOLS AND CHARMS—BULLET PROOF—STONE OF THE EARTH—NKASA.

AFTER a long, tedious journey from Wyoming Territory to Boston, a voyage from New York to Glasgow, another voyage from Liverpool to Banana and Matadi; thence overland to Palabala—how refreshing it was to sit down at the mission station to rest awhile! Here in the very good society of several brethren I remained for a month. There are about thirty boys and girls living at this station, and each night at eight they met for prayers. One of the brethren would read the Scriptures in the Ki-kongo language, and pray in the same tongue. The children themselves would unite very heartily in singing some translations of Sankey's hymns. One little fellow, whose heart the Lord had touched, could scarcely sing at all. He had the sleeping sickness, and as I looked at him, while the other children were singing "Yimbilanga kiesi, kiesi" (Singing glory, glory), I thought, he will soon be in that other and better land, "singing glory, glory." Not long afterward, little Johnny was called away, to sing, I believe, around the throne of God in heaven. This little boy, like the others, had been rescued from heathenism, and clothed, and fed—better still, had been told of the love of God through Christ Jesus our Lord.

In wandering around, I found evidences of superstition on every hand. At the entrance to every town, there is generally a kind of mound or structure which is intended to keep the "Ndoki" (evil spirit) away. It is very certain from the frequent "palavers," that he is *not* kept away. I frequently noticed a small branch of a tree, tied near a doorway or in the entrance to their houses. The purpose of this is to keep away "yevi," or thieves. I have noticed that they knot the grass near their sweet potato patches, and this is likewise a protection against thieves. The entrance to each house was also guarded by a number of "minkisi," or idols.

So great was the superstition in some towns, that I could not take out my pocket book to make notes, without exciting the suspicion of the people. It is also a common practice to kill a fowl, and to scatter its blood and feathers on and across the chief pathways leading to the towns. This again is to prevent the admission of evil. From inquiries made, I fail to discover any reasonable explanation for this, and it has probably no connection whatever with the passover and the sprinkling of blood. Having no literature of any kind, their traditional records are of questionable value and authenticity; for their statements of events that took place not more than a generation ago are confused and unreliable.

One Sunday I accompanied Mr. Banks into a native village, where he tried to hold the attention of the people for a while in telling them of Jesus and his love. One man was interested in me, and with little regard for the preacher, pointed to my whiskers, and exclaimed: "What fine, long whiskers he has got!" Another, observing my spectacles, remarked: "See! they are tied with a string. If they fall, they will not be broken." A third person, a great tall fellow, was busily sharpening a huge knife, and presently took himself off to tap palm trees.

One of our missionaries had occasion to visit a town

in which there was a sick child, and while there a "nganga," or witch doctor, came to him. The "nganga" had a large bunch of shells behind his head, and said they would give him power to catch the devil and kill him. My friend asked him:

"Did you ever see the devil?"

"Ve" (No).

"Can any one see him?"

"No, white man."

"Then how can you kill him? Your fetich is nonsense; your shells have no power, and you only do these things to get cloth and frighten the people."

"I can kill men with these charms."

"Kill me, then."

"Oh, you are a white man."

"I am the same as you, and if you cannot kill me, you can kill no one."

The "nganga" took himself off, looking very sheepish.

"Their land is full of idols" may be said of Congo, or rather of that part of it known as the Cataract region and the Lower Congo. Fetichism and superstition prevail, not only on the Lower Congo, but all along the west coast of Africa. So far as the Congo country, is known, however, idols, or "minkisi," are confined to the Cataract region. The natives who live near the coast have more "charms" than those who live in the interior. How are we to account for this? We firmly believe that the Roman Catholics, who, three hundred years ago, planted their standard on the lower river, are largely responsible for the introduction of idols.

Mr. Grenfell says: "So far back as the close of the sixteenth century, San Salvador, the capital of the kingdom of Congo was a walled city and could boast of its cathedral and seven other churches. It was the see of a bishop (at one time filled by a native), and till the middle of the seventeenth century the rites of the Roman Catholic Church were regularly maintained. So far back as two hundred and thirty years ago, the country was partially civilized, and had become nominally Christian. But after the transference of the see to St. Paul de Loando, and after the removal of the military force of the Portuguese government, the churches fell into ruins, and people lapsed into barbarism; for, while the rites of the Roman Catholic Church are well calculated to appeal to the native mind, they very evidently fail to accomplish the real changes of heart and life which characterize a vital Christianity."

Some years ago, a Jesuit missionary presented a little crucifix to a Congo chief. This crucifix was afterward exhibited in great glee to a Protestant missionary.

" What is that?" asked the missionary.

"An ' nkisi,' white man."

" Where did you obtain it?"

"A white man gave it to me."

And so the chief rejoiced in the addition to his idols. Whatever instruction the Jesuit missionary gave the chief respecting the crucifix was forgotten. The idol alone remained. There do remain traces of the Roman Church, but not a trace of good. Is there not an evident connection between the images and crucifixes introduced in the Lower Congo three hundred years ago and the fetich idols so highly prized by the unenlightened Congo native? Would not the superstitious native be only too ready to appropriate this new form of fetichism? Why are idols so numerous on the lower river, and so seldom found on the upper river? Mr. McKittick, who lived at our Equator station, and where I lived six months, says: "The word 'nkisi' (idol) on the lower river means 'dumb' among these people. It is my firm belief that they had no idols in the Cataract region previous to the introduction of Roman Catholicism. I have never yet met with one anywhere in the interior, and, after making inquiries, cannot find a trace of any."

Be that as it may, there are many fetich idols on the lower river. Unlike the natives of some heathen lands, the Congo people do not *worship* their idols, nor do they, so far as I am aware, ever pray to them. They are really not objects of worship, but are used as charms, as means of protection in time of danger, and to ward off evil spirits. Some instances of the absurd superstition of the Congo natives may well provoke a smile.

A native of the Cataract region said to a friend of mine:

"This 'nkisi,' white man, will protect me from the guns of my enemies."

"Where did you get it?"

"From the 'nganga.'"

"Do you always carry it with you?"

"Yes. If I have an enemy who wishes to shoot me, he cannot injure me while I carry my 'nkisi.'"

"Where do you carry it?"

"Here on my breast."

"See here; I will show you that it cannot protect you from my rifle. Look here; I will give you these 'malensua' (handkerchiefs) if you will consent to stand twenty yards away, and allow me to fire at your breast, while it is covered by your 'nkisi.'" The native cast a greedy glance at the bright-colored handkerchiefs, but refused to face the white man's gun, although he still insisted that his "nkisi" would render his swarthy breast bullet proof.

Another kind of idol used by these deluded people, is called "nzadi a nsi," or stone of the earth. It is of two parts, composed of one small idol and a wooden rattle. In the hands of the witch doctor, or "nganga," it is thought to be of great value. I once obtained one, and desired a converted native to tell me all about it, together with several others. I asked:

"What is the purpose of this 'nkisi'?"

"I will tell you. When any one is accused of causing the death of any person, it is believed that this 'nzadi a nsi' will enable them to find out the guilty person."

"In what way? These are only two pieces of wood."

"The 'nganga' will call all the people together. They will stand in a circle, while the 'nganga' walks around and looks into the face of each person, at the same time shaking the rattle and holding the small idol close to his ear. After awhile he selects his victim, and pretends that the idol spoke in his ear, and told him of the guilty person."

"But do the people believe all this?"

"Most of them have believed in the power of the 'nganga'; but now the 'mindele mia Nzambi' (white men of God) are here, many will listen to the words of the white man."

"But surely the 'nganga' do not believe in all this; they surely know better?"

"They do know it is wrong, but they do it to get plenty of cloth."

"Did you believe in the 'nzadi a nsi'?"

"I did before the white man of God came."

"Do you still believe the 'nganga' has any power?"

"No; he is false and knows better."

The persons selected by the "nganga" in such cases, are generally those who have accumulated a little cloth, or it may be some one against whom he has a grudge, or it may be some infirm woman, who is no longer able to till the soil, to plant peanuts, or to make "kwanga."

Those who are pointed out by the "nganga-ngombo," or witch doctor, as criminals, have to submit to the final test of drinking "nkasa" (poison). This they are always willing to do. They know they are innocent, and believe that therefore they will not suffer. Others may have suffered great agony and died, but, of course, *they were guilty.* Many of the natives will not admit that it is a poison, although it is a rank poison.

If a person takes "nkasa" and escapes, he is greatly honored. The "nganga" can regulate the quantity and the quality of the "nkasa." That is, he can, if he choose, give a small quantity, well diluted, so that the person may vomit and recover, or he may give so large a quantity of the strong poison as to make recovery impossible.

If time be given to the condemned one, he will usually fast, so as to be in a better condition to vomit after taking the poison. At least, it is their opinion that an empty stomach is favorable to the rejection of the poison. It very frequently proves fatal.

No word of sympathy reaches the ear of the dying one, but taunts and jeers are heard on every side. They mimic the contortions produced by the sufferer in the agonies of death. They challenge him to stand upon his feet. It is to them a time of fiendish pleasure, though they know not how soon one of themselves may be called to drink the fatal cup.

"Ha, if you are not 'ndoki' (possessed of a devil), stand up."

"Why do you not speak if you are innocent?"

Sometimes they terminate the sufferings of the dying one by throwing him into the fire, by strangling, by drowning, or with the knife.

## CHAPTER VI.

KANGA MPAKA—ORNAMENTS ON THE GRAVES—EMBALMING HIS BODY—"HOLELY" ORNAMENTS—IS IT WRONG TO STEAL—CAN HE SEE SPIRITS?

IN the early history of the mission, one of our brethren had an amusing little experience at Palabala. The chief of the town, old Kanga Mpaka, had been very encroaching for some time. One day he came around, and after taking the cloth due as wages for two boys who worked at the station, he wanted some for a little girl named Ikwangu. This little girl was not only very young, and unable to do anything, but had also a frightful ulcer on her right foot, which seemed to defy all medical treatment. The poor little girl had been, of course, nothing but an expense to the mission. He also wanted cloth for Frank, a boy about eight, and also "chop" for himself. That is, he wanted to be clothed and fed at the expense of the mission. Our missionary pretended to be quite out of patience with him. Old Kanga Mpaka kept very cool and silent, and after awhile left. Next morning the little girl was sent for to leave the station and go home, which she did, and shortly afterward a whole gang of "kapitas" came and wanted to know why the missionary had accused the king of stealing, and what he had stolen. Our missionary was completely mystified and asked them to explain. It appears that he had rapped the table several times with his knuckles while remonstrating with the old chief, and this, to the mind of the Ki-kongo native, was an accusation of theft. With some difficulty our friend persuaded the "kapitas" of his innocence, and a cup of coffee all round put the matter all right. A "dash" to the old king smoothed things over, and he was soon on good terms again.

In some parts of Africa they bury their dead beneath the floor of the native hut, but in Congo they generally bury them in some secluded part of the jungle, and near to their town. As a rule, however, they do not bury them for a good while, but they are kept for a considerable period. Of course, the length of time their bodies are preserved unburied depends upon the rank and position they held. An ordinary, poor individual, might not be kept more than a week or two, whereas the body of a chief is commonly preserved for a year. Old Kanga Mpaka, of Palabala, died in 1886. His body was preserved for many months. During his lifetime, the old man had accumulated much cloth and other riches. He had also about twelve wives, and was considered quite an important chief or king. His death caused great commotion. One thousand guns were fired, and five or six huge ivory horns were blown vigorously in token of mourning for the dead chief. His poor old body was embalmed, or, more properly speaking, it was smoked in one of his huts. A large quantity of the cloth he had accumulated was wrapped around the corpse. It was then suspended by cords to the roof of the hut. A slow fire was constantly kept burning underneath, until the body was shriveled and dried up.

The wives sat in this hut for a part of the time, mourning and lamenting their loss. After keeping his corpse for a long time, it was buried with great honor and ceremony and firing of guns. About a year before he died, his successor was formally recognized, at which ceremony I happened to be present. This ceremony of appointing and acknowledging his successor occupied some time, and took place in front of the king's "lumbu" (king's house), in the midst of a drizzling rain.

On this occasion, palm wine and other intoxicants, alas! were not wanting, and several neighboring chiefs, by their peculiar yelling and dancing, gave evidence that they were *not quite* sober.

Poor old Kanga Mpaka. Cunning, shrewd, old fellow, he had often heard the gospel in his old age, but rejected it, and died as he lived, without God and without hope. I think I can see his knavish look as he visited the mission to open up some palaver or dispute. His attitude was most striking, as, with snuff box in one hand, and stick in the other, his legs encircled with brass rings, a handsome military coat on, and a piece of blue silk tied around his head, he poured forth a perfect torrent of words. What powers of oratory the old man possessed! How skillfully he could plead his cause, wright or wrong—generally wrong! No doubt his grave has by this time been covered with ornaments, for this is the custom at Palabala.

On the edge of the "nfinda" (forest), 'neath the shade of graceful palm trees, or the overhanging branches of the huge baobab, in a spot where the evil spirits have been scared by the firing of guns and consecrated by the superstitious rites of the " nganga," they bury their dead.

Wrapped in cloth, and secured by the fibre of the palm tree, they bury the smoked, shriveled and dried-up remains, in a grave about four feet deep, while those that are alive and remain give vent to the fear and sorrow of their heart in a very demonstrative manner.

On the top of the mound they place bottles, jugs, dishes, wash-basins, large earthenware of different kinds, as also demijohns. All these are empty, and if the traveler will cautiously approach and dare to examine them, he will find that each article has a hole in the bottom.

I asked a native who was with me when I visited some graves:

" Why do you break holes in all the things you put on the ' minkala'? " (graves.)

" Yevi, mindele (thieves, white man). We break holes in them, and then no one will steal them."

" Would the people steal them if they were in good condition?"

"Inga, mindele" (Yes, white man).

"Why do you put all these things on the graves?"

"Perhaps the spirits of those who are buried here might want them."

"Don't you think it is very wrong to steal?"

"Yes, ka mbote ko" (It is not good).

"Then why do you steal?"

"It is very wrong, *if we are caught.*"

"Why do you shoot over and around the grave when you bury?"

"To frighten away the 'mpevi yambi'" (bad spirits).

"Do you really think you can drive them all away?"

"Yes, power is with the 'nganga.' He can do it. 'Lenda kwandi'" (can really).

"Why do you think there are evil spirits around the graves?"

"Sometimes the 'nganga' can see them."

"You must not believe the 'nganga'; he tells lies to get plenty of cloth. But why are you so much afraid of evil spirits?"

"They come and steal our spirits, white man, when

we die; they stole the spirits of those whom we have buried."

"The 'nganga' told you that, and he does not tell the truth. Can the 'nganga' really drive evil spirits away from the town?"

"Yes. 'Kedika kwandi'" (truth verily).

"They are deceiving you. Do you not see that the 'ngangas' themselves die?"

"Yes, perhaps their 'nkisi' was not powerful enough to keep them."

"No, it was not. The 'ngangas' die, and they can not prevent any one from dying when 'Mzambi Mpungu' calls" (When Great God calls).

"The white man speaks wisely."

"Do not your goats and sheep die?"

"They die."

"Do not your 'zinsusu' (fowls) die?"

"Yes, white man."

"Do not elephants die after living many seasons? the animals die? the fish die? the birds die?"

"True, 'mindele.'"

"Then why should not we die the same as do goats and sheep, and fowls, and elephants, and birds, and fishes? Look at your forests; do not the leaves decay, and others take their place? Does not the grass wither? Do not all flowers fade? After working and planting, and hunting, and building, and eating, and sleeping for many seasons, do you feel the same? Can you climb the palm tree as when you were a young man? Do your fathers feel strong to chase the elephant and buffalo as in former days?"

"The white man speaks words of wisdom."

"The 'ngangas' cannot help you. They themselves are often sick, and they, too, die. They cannot do you any good. 'Nzambi Mpungu kaka kuna dizulu' (the Great God only in heaven) can help us to live, and make us ready to die."

# CHAPTER VII.

JIGGERS—STEAMSHIP CORISCO—TAKING MEDICINE—SOUND OF
THE DRUM—THE ORCHESTRA—THE NGANGA SAYS IT MAY.

WHILE at Palabala I had my first experience with jiggers. The "nvidi," or jigger, was originally imported from Brazil. In size it is small, almost invisible. It is carried to the various mission stations by the natives, who have usually a large number in their feet. This is especially true in the dry season, when, for a number of months, there is no rain. During that period they increase with astonishing rapidity. The rainy season, however, almost exterminates them. Up to this time I had very vague ideas as to what a jigger really was. I certainly thought it was sufficiently large to be easily seen. The jigger has a great fondness for the feet. The reason of this is, I suppose, because the feet are next to the earth, and these insectile invaders can more easily reach the feet than any other part of one's body. During the dry season, our children need constant attention, or their feet would be in a sorry plight. It is a singular fact that few of our younger mission children will take the proper precautions to keep their feet free from these pests. This is partly because they do not like the short, but rather painful operation of extracting them, and partly from a foolish unconcern. Some of the little native boys are very skillful in removing them. The only surgical instrument they use is a small pointed stick. The jigger invariably burrows under the toe nails, and when it has fairly (or unfairly) forced itself under the skin, it immediately encloses itself in a bag, in which it lays its eggs. If neglected, it will increase in astonishing numbers, and in a short time will eat away the tissue, and destroy the toe. At first, and for some time, they do not cause much pain. The only indication of their presence is a slight feeling of discomfort, as though the toes had chafed by walking, accompanied by an occasional prickly sensation. In probing, great caution is necessary to avoid rupturing the bag in which insect and eggs are enclosed. This the Congo boy knows how to do with as much tact and skill as any surgeon.

When I had been at Palabala about a month, I felt one night an uncomfortable sensation in the toes of both feet. I was sitting at the time on my bed, dressed in my "pyjamas." The thought occurred to me that I was perhaps a prey to jiggers. So I called to Mr. C.:

"Oh, Mr. C., I think the jiggers have bored all through my toes."

"I told you you would get them, walking about without your shoes."

It was even so. My friend came, smiling all over his face. An examination proved that there were just seven of these small annoyances seeking to live in my feet.

My friend very deftly removed them, and ever after I was very careful to get my boy to make a daily inspection of my "understandings."

About this time, and while I was preparing to go up country, some important news reached our mission. The beautiful steamer the "Corisco," bound from Liverpool to the southwest coast of Africa, was wrecked on the Kru coast, and was a total loss. She struck a hidden rock about four o'clock in the morning, and went down in twenty minutes, the passengers having barely time to escape into their boats in their night clothing. A portion of her cargo was for our mission. There was also some clothing on board for me. The "Corisco" left Liverpool three weeks after the "Kinsembo," in which I sailed, and belonged to the same company. Among the passengers on this steamer was a young missionary who was bound for Old Calabar. When I sailed on the "Kinsembo," I was the only missionary on board.

Mrs. H. G. Guinness, of London, urged me to wait and go by the "Corisco" for the sake of Christian companionship. I was anxious, however, to get up the Congo before the rainy season commenced, and so, much though I desired the presence of a brother missionary during the long voyage, I decided to go alone. When I heard of the loss of the "Corisco," how thankful I was that I did not take passage in that ill-fated steamer!

Among the passengers on board this latter steamer was old Oko Jumbo, one of the Bonny kings He had made a visit to London to see an oculist.

Among the cargo there were thirty-three bags of

rice for our mission. There was also about two hundred and seventy-five dollars in English gold, which was to pay our carpenters from Acra, their time having expired.

About this time there was a great scene in the neighborhood of our mission. About two hundred yards from our station, there is a small village, of which Nikiangila is the worthy chief. Nikiangila rules over but few people, but on any important occasion they can easily attract the natives of other towns. A big dance, plenty of palm wine, or, it may be, something stronger, in connection with a big "nkisi palaver" or fetich charm, is irresistible. Such practices undoubtedly affect their health very seriously, for these dances and fetichisms are indulged in for several days at one time, with scarcely any intermission for rest. Like Kanga Mpaka, Nikiangila rejoiced in several wives. For a long time he suffered from a very diseased breast, which was a mass of sores, made all the worse by foolish attempts to heal it by fetichism. As a last recourse, one of his wives determined to take the fetich potions herself, in the hope that the "nkisi" might work through her, and that Nikiangila might thus be healed. The appointed day arrived, and natives came from all around to take part in the fetich dance, and to sympathize with the old chief. In front of his house a space was cleared, a small fire was kindled, and the fetich potion was prepared. In the centre, and on the outside of a large circle, there were several drums. These were the only instruments of music (?) used in connection with the dance. The native drums are of various shapes and sizes. One of these was the trunk of a small tree, hollowed out, about ten feet in length, and with goatskin tightly stretched over the one end. It is astonishing what noise can be gotten out of these "zingoma," or drums. The native who beats the drum, and thus guides and controls the dancers' movements, has great powers of endurance, to say the least of it. The drum itself is laid along the ground, with a piece of wood under the end to which the skin is attached. The drummer sits astride of the intsrument, and his hands are the drum sticks. It is not every one who can do this properly. I attempted in vain to imitate the drummer, but I only succeeded in producing shouts of laughter on the part of the bystanders. Every movement of the dancers, as well as their song, is regulated by the beat of the drummer. The "nganga" or doctor of fetich, figures conspicuously in ceremonies like these. He of all others does not like interferences on the part of the white man. It is he who prepares the fetich potions. After a large number of natives had assembled in front of the old chief's house, the poor wife who was going to take the fetich medicine appeared on the scene. She was an object of interest to the chief, to his other wives, and to the people, who came to contribute to the interest of the occasion. What the medicine actually was I could not discover. Its medicinal properties were probably very inferior. They attach more importance to it as a *charm* than as an actual medicinal remedy. Sitting upon a mat on the ground, and surrounded by the old chief and his other wives, the noble wife took the bitter draught that was to heal the sores on her husband's neck and breast. This chief doubtlessly felt fortunate in having such a wife. After taking the medicine, her wriggling and contortions of countenance were sickening to behold. Not that the medicine was affecting her in this manner; for we asked:

"Is the medicine poison?"

"No, 'mundele,' it is not poison."

"Then why does the woman make all those movements?"

"Oh, it is the 'nkisi' that is working."

"Is all that going to heal Nikiangila?"

"The 'nganga' says it will do him good."

"Why does not Nikiangila take the medicine?"

"Oh, his wife wanted to take it. It will do the same good, the 'nganga' says."

"But the 'nganga' has tried before, and failed."

"Oh, yes, white man; but this is a very powerful 'nkisi' and will do good."

After the woman took the medicine, the dancers commenced their somewhat awkward movements, to the sound of the drum. This was continued with little intermission for several days. During the night season, the dancing was more vigorous than by day, while under the influence of stale palm wine they yelled and shouted most lustily. While some rested, others took their places, and it was vain to seek sleep within a quarter of a mile. Occasionally a chief would step into the ring or circle, and this would incite the dancers to greater gyrations. Toward the close of the third day, the interest began to flag. The powerful fetich had failed to produce the desired effect. The poor wife was quite exhausted. The old chief was no better. We were glad when it came to an end, as we knew what the result would be. After this the old chief came to our mission station, and was treated repeatedly by our brethren. At one time, under their treatment, he seemed almost cured, but the sores appeared again in their most malignant form. Soon after the mission was established at Palabala, Nikiangila exhibited great interest in the story of the cross. But when, later on, he discovered that the gospel and fetichism could not harmonize, he attended less frequently, and sometimes for months he would not be seen at any of our services. I shall never forget the big dances at Nikiangila's. In imagination, I can still hear the horrid shouts and yells of the people, as they were dancing, and having a special time with their "nkisi."

## CHAPTER VIII.

IN CAMP—CHOP BOXES—ROUSING THE CAMP—BAD PEOPLE—
CONQUERED BUT NOT SUBDUED—THE LUVU—BANZA MANTEKE
—LITTLE JOHNNY—UNDER A VOW—SMOKING THE BODY—THE
NKIMBA—THE SACRED GROVE—INTRUDING—NDOKI.

ON September 7, 1885, my companion and myself took our departure from the Palabala plateau, bound for Mukimbungu. We had with us nine men and three boys, to carry our goods, tent, beds, and food. The descent of the hill or plateau was carefully made. For the first few miles up the country from Palabala it is probably one of the roughest roads in the country. Immediately before we commenced the descent, we obtained a partial view of the Yelala Falls, and long afterward we could still hear the mighty cataract, like the rumbling of distant thunder.

Our first stopping place was the "Maza ma nkenge" stream. This name signifies something like "waters of bitterness." A market is held near this stream every fourth day. The market is known as "Nkenge Elamba." We halted here only a short time, and after lunch we proceeded onward. This day's marching was very fatiguing on account of the tall grass and the rough, sharp quartz.

Early in the afternoon we arrived at the Nduzi or Luiza stream, and here we determined to pitch our tent. The first day's marching is always trying, and we were both in an exhausted condition.

Two men were told off to fix the tent; a third was despatched to gather kindling wood, while one of our men who acted as cook explored the depths of our boxes of food, or "chop boxes" as they are popularly called. Some tall grass was removed, a space was cleared, the ground swept, and the tent erected. It was pitched toward the sunrising and near to the north bank of the stream.

Just as the sun sank into the far west, the fire was kindled, and the crackling wood and the smoke and light were a pleasing contrast to the sombre background of trees and grass. For a few moments after the sun went down, there was perfect stillness. I hoped that this might continue, but I was grievously disappointed; for, before darkness fairly set in, there was every evidence that we should have a wakeful

Life and Scenes in Congo.    FOREST AND RIVER LIFE.    Page 155.

night. In vain did we make every effort to keep the mosquitoes out of our tent. In vain did we repel their advances. The cry was "Still they come," and they came. We utterly failed to secure "balmy sleep," and, indeed, any kind of sleep. Nor were the mosquitoes the only disturbers. Frogs croaked; various birds screeched and screamed; grasshoppers loudly chirped; and what with the insects and discordant music, we could hardly be other than feverish in the morning.

Before the sun peeped into our tent, we had risen, and roused the sleeping camp. I say sleeping camp, for myself and friend were probably the only ones who were really disturbed. So we called :

" O Kuzielo " (O cook).

" Yes, masta."

" Light fire one time " (Light fire at once).

" Small bit fire live, masta." (In plainer English that would mean, "There is a little fire.")

" Well, make coffee quick, then we go."

" Yes, masta."

A cup of coffee has a wonderful effect, and, after a sweet season of communion with God, we began our march.

The movements of the carriers are apt to be slow and undecided the first thing in the morning. So it is necessary to superintend everything; otherwise something will surely be left behind.

"Now you boys, pack them tent good. That no be proper. Pick up that rope. Don't leave them pegs."

These and other such remarks are necessary before a satisfactory start can be made.

Our route was over the Ekongo di Elemba hill or plateau, which is nearly fifteen hundred feet high. In some places the grass had been burned for several miles, and we were quite blackened by passing through it; in other places, the roads were made well-nigh impassable by the tall grass, which frequently reaches a height of sixteen feet, or more. It would be a very serious matter to get lost in this grass. On the summit of Ekongo di Elemba there is a town of considerable size, the people of which had a very bad reputation. They had contracted, alas! a liking for the white man's strong drink, which was supplied by the traders on the lower river, and others. Travelers through the town were frequently interrupted and annoyed, and cases of theft were common. Carriers were prevented from passing up the country with their loads.

At last, very severe measures were taken by the officials of the Congo Free State. The town was burned to ashes and several people killed. This took place in 1886. I passed down the country immediately afterward, while yet it was a heap of smoking, blackened ruins. Houses or huts in Congo, however, are easily rebuilt or replaced. The people of Ekongo di Elemba were conquered but not subdued; for, abandoning their burning homes, they went to a more isolated spot in a valley a few miles away.

From Ekongo di Elemba we descended to the Bembizi stream, a miserable apology for a river. Just beyond this there is another stream or torrent bed, called Nkama Nsoki. After lunch, we prepared ourselves for another climb to the town of Mazamba. There are few towns along the line of travel between Palabala and Banza Manteke. The town of Mazamba no longer exists; for, like Ekongo di Elemba, it has gone up in smoke and flame. Immediately beyond the site of the town, there is an immense forest known to white travelers as the Mazamba wood. This wood is the home of the leopard and other wild animals, and it took us fully half an hour to thread our way through it.

It was necessary to look well to one's feet, as the spreading roots of trees frequently crossed the path, just an inch or two above the ground. Tangled creepers, too, made it difficult for our men to pass along with their loads, which they invariably carry on their heads. Trees rent asunder by the lightning and storm, or killed by the united attacks of white ants, were fallen across the path, and our men, with their hatchets, had to cut a passage around them.

The change from the painful glare of the sun to the deep shade of the Mazamba forest was most grateful and refreshing. Emerging again into the light of day, we continued our march for about twenty-five minutes, which brought us to the Luvu River. This is a beautiful stream of clear, cool water. At this time it was fordable, but during the rainy season the river is deep and powerful, and travelers have to wait several days, it may be, to get across. In traveling during the wet season, it is always wise to cross the stream near to which the tent is to be pitched for the night. The reason of this is, though the stream may be fordable, a storm may come on before the morning, and effectually prevent a passage. Various attempts have been made to construct a rude swing bridge over this river, but they have invariably failed, as the structures have been swept away. Here we arranged for the night, and I fell into a deep sleep, from which I was only awakened by the repeated efforts of my friend. Whether the insect life was less abundant in this valley; whether frogs were less numerous or better behaved; whether the night-flying goatsucker uttered his plaintive cries elsewhere, I cannot determine, for I slept, and slept soundly.

On the following morning, four and a half hours' march brought us to Banza Manteke.

There is very little good traveling between Palabala and this place. It is really a series of precipitous hills, immense grassy plains, and impenetrable jungle. Banza Manteke, however, is well situated, and the mission is planted in the centre of a number of towns. This mission station, which was built and established by Mr. Richards, was for some years a most discouraging place. At no place in the Cataract region had fetichism, and all forms of evil, taken a deeper root apparently than at Banza Manteke. To give one instance out of many: At our Lukungu Station, about two hundred and thirty miles from the coast, and one hundred and ten miles from Palabala, we have, as at all our stations, a mission school. Most of the children who attend it live at the station. Some have been engaged to assist in the many little duties of the mission, such as cleaning the rooms, waiting at table, and washing dishes. Others have been ransomed in various parts of the country, and they stay at the mission, as they have no other friends, and no other home. Among these children, there is one wee boy, a bright-eyed, thin-lipped, pretty little fellow, and his name is Johnny. He has been at this mission the greater part of his short life, and is full of interest to its inmates.

Johnny was very fond of peanuts. We had a small patch of peanuts in our garden, and sometimes I would meet Johnny going in that direction, and knowing his errand, I would ask, speaking in English:

"Where are you going, Johnny?"

Johnny would invariably reply in Ki-kongo, and that in a whisper:

"Kuna zinguba" (to the peanuts).

"Well, Johnny, don't eat too many."

Johnny (softly), "Yes."

When Johnny was a tiny babe, his mother lived at Banza Manteke, where Mr. Richards has been laboring so successfully for a number of years.

A king died at Banza Manteke, and after three months had passed this poor woman was accused of causing his death. Of course, she was quite innocent. Mavuzi, one of our mission boys, was in the town, and he discovered that they were about to murder the poor creature. They were making a great noise in the town, as Mavuzi rushed up to the mission station, crying:

"Oh, 'mundele,' they are going to kill a woman and her child."

"What for, Mavuzi?"

"Oh, they say she is 'ndoki,' and that she caused the death of the king."

Mr. Richards and Mr. W. at once started off for the town, hoping to be able to rescue the poor woman and her babe. The first thing they saw was a hut full of women, who were crying as if in an awful agony. Mr. Richards asked :

" Where is the woman whom they want to kill ? "

With a shriek they rushed out of the hut, and made for the woods, crying :

" We are under a vow to the ' minkisi ' " (or idols).

Further inquiries were made to no effect, as everybody replied :

" Ka tu zaidi ko " (we don't know). Although everybody knew where she was.

Mr. Richards did all he could to find out where the murderers had gone, but without success. Next day he learned that they had taken the woman and her child some miles away, where first shooting the mother, they then cut her throat, nearly severing the head from the body. The man appointed to perform the horrid task took the child and dashed it to the ground ; but a woman who was present, who had some feeling in her bosom, snatched up the child, and ran away. After considerable trouble and effort, Mr. Richards obtained possession of the tiny babe. It was tenderly cared for, and Mr. Richards wrote :

" We hope and pray the boy may grow up and teach his people better things." Will not my readers echo that prayer?

The body of the king on whose account this precious life was sacrificed was not buried for a long time. Deaths and murders were interesting events to the people, and they were fully occupied firing guns, beating drums, and yelling by day and by night, for some time. The dead body was encased in many rolls of cloth and mats, and hung up over a slow fire, and well smoked. Mr. Richards was in the village one Sunday, but on account of this horrible custom was quite unable to stay.

In those days Banza Manteke was the stronghold of the " nkimba." The " nkimba " is a sort of priesthood, or rather a kind of secret order or society among the Ba-kongo people. After being initiated into the "nkimba" fellowship, they profess to be transformed to live another life, and speak another language. We once saw the "nkimba" at Palabala. Their faces were covered with a generous supply of white clay, which gave to them a strangely hideous appearance, and they passed us without any recognition whatever. This was not from any lack of respect, as the natives of the Cataract region are ordinarily respectful.

The glorious work at Banza Manteke has largely interfered with the sacred order of the "Nkimba." One day, soon after our Mr. Richards had established himself at Banza Manteke, he started off after breakfast, with several boys, to visit some villages. The first, Banza Vala, to the southwest of the mission, was empty; the people had all gone away to market. Proceeding, he came to Ndambo, which was the "minkisi" village, about a mile from the mission station. Knowing that this place was Satan's seat, Mr. Richards determined to stay and observe their practices, if possible. The men caught hold of him, and tried to prevent his entering the village, but he pushed on. The boys who were with him became so frightened that they ran away and hid themselves in the grass. All adult males have to go through a training, which is to initiate them into their superstitious and diabolical rites. They take a year in this training, and do not wash during all that time. They had an enclosure made of the stems of palm leaves and huts built inside. Mr. Richards determined to get inside, which he did, and saw many of the "nkimba" dressed in their peculiar costume. It is made of grass and palm branches split. A round flat piece, four feet in diameter, woven into a basket shape, and having a hole in the centre large enough to pass over the head, rests horizontally on the shoulder; a tube a foot deep is made long enough to go over the head, and fasten on to the circle, holes being made in the tube to look through, and feathers being placed on the top. Around the flat, target-shaped piece is a deep fringe of soft broad loose grass. When they have on this affair, nothing of the body is seen except the legs, which are painted white. There was nothing else in the enclosure, save some drums and a gun.

At the next two villages the people were also gone to the market, and Mr. Richards felt somewhat disappointed that there was no opportunity of speaking to the people. Proceeding onward, in another half hour, he came to a large village, called Kuindemba. Here there was a lot of men, women, and children, drumming, yelling, and dancing around a poor woman who was suffering probably from rheumatism. Seeing a white man, they became silent and angry, and wanted to know what he had come for.

"To teach you about God, and how to worship him."

"We don't know him, and we don't want to know him, or worship him: go away, white man."

"What is the matter with that woman? What are you doing to her?"

"Nothing, nothing, nothing."

"Yes, you are trying to make her well."

She was sitting on a mat all alone at this time.

"You are not going the right way to do it."

"'Ndoki' has made her ill; we were trying to make her well."

"But this is a foolish way to try; listen to me."

"No, we will not listen; go away, white man."

They grew quite angry; but, unconsciously to themselves, they at last became somewhat interested in his words regarding the works of God. After telling them the story of the six days' work of creation, and after describing each day's work, they were asked, "Why not worship him who made all these good things?"

The question, "Who makes your food grow?" seemed especially to interest them, and they acknowledged that God made everything. Again they were asked, "Why not worship him?" There was a grunt of approval from many. They were then told about Christ the Redeemer, and asked to close their eyes during a short prayer, in which the sick woman was remembered. A thunderstorm then came on, and our friend, Mr. Richards, had to return home as quickly as possible.

# CHAPTER IX.

A GREAT CHANGE—CHURCH BELLS—OPPOSITION—NEVER RETURNED—WILLING TO SUFFER—I GO BACK—CLIMBING THE PALM TREE.

THE events referred to in the latter part of the last chapter occurred some years ago. Since then what a great and mighty change has taken place in and around Banza Manteke! One can but exclaim, "Oh, change! stupendous change!" In 1886, I passed through Banza Manteke, and witnessed a scene such as seldom falls to the lot of man. A revival had broken out. For years Mr. Richards had toiled without any visible results. Seed was sown, but there was little or no harvest. His faith was sorely tried; but he determined to make a more vigorous effort. In God's own time the blessing came. On my arrival, I found Richards carrying on a service that had already lasted several hours. The house, the entry, and the approaches all around the station were well-nigh thronged by people, most of whom were in evident anxiety about their souls. Within the house, some were prostrate on the floor, some on their knees calling upon God, while some who had already found Christ were themselves trying to lead others into the light, thus immediately becoming missionaries themselves.

As we approached the mission, we were met by several of the natives, and the unusal warm grasp of their hands, and the joyful expression of their faces, assured me, even before I asked, that they had found joy and peace in believing. During the whole of this blessed season of grace, Richards scarcely found time to eat. From morning until noon, and from noon until the evening, he was busy preaching the word, dealing with inquirers, and treating the sick. Now that they had lost faith in their "minkisi" and "zinganga" they wanted to be treated by the white man. They had faith in the gospel which he preached, and they now began to have confidence in the medical skill of the preacher. Many who but a short time before this were apparently indifferent were now completely conquered by the power of the word. It was a scene never to be forgotten. A Swedish traveler who visited Banza Manteke soon afterward, thus wrote: " I was rather tired when I reached the top of the hill above Banza Manteke. I was changed in a moment, when I saw below, in a bird's eye view, the pretty villages and green ravines. The tones of a bell greeted me, and the whole impression was one of peace. I was not wrong. Arriving at the mission, I could not believe my eyes. I found Mr. Richards preaching in the middle of a large circle of men and women, who were throwing away their "minkisi" or idols. That is to say, I have been witness to an event of great importance; and Banza Manteke will be distinguished in the future Congo history as the first Christian parish, to-day numbering many hundreds."

It must not be supposed, however, that all the people were favorable to the reception of the gospel. On the contrary, many were steadily and bitterly opposed to it from the very beginning. First among these were the witch-doctors or "zinganga." Like Demetrius of old, their craft was in danger, and while they knew they were all acting the part of impostors, yet they professed to be in earnest, and to be greatly alarmed. These men would naturally expect to lose their supply of cloth, for if the people became Christians and gave up their "minkisi," the "ngangas" would have to turn their attention to something else. Hence the missionary could not count on the sympathy of the "zinganga." Nor were these the only opposers, for many of the chiefs in the neighboring towns were most jealous of the missionaries' influence. The preaching of the word struck at the root of many of their sinful practices. Most of these chiefs were polygamists, and they also encouraged and sustained a sort of domestic slavery. They began to see that this gospel would antagonize many of their interests. Then, too, they entertained very ridiculous notions of the Kingship of Christ. Like Herod of old, they imagined that this Jesus would detract from their own power and authority. Though friendly at the first, they at length began to watch the missionaries with jealousy and suspicion. Hence, as the number of converts increased, the opposition of the "zinganga" and the chiefs became pronounced. Some of the new converts were tempted and tried in various ways; sometimes by ridicule, sometimes by threatening, and at other times by endeavoring to allure them back to their former practices. Rarely, however, did they succeed, for the converts were immovable. Immediately after their conversion, they gave evidence of it by their abundant labors for God. So far as they were able, they preached the gospel which they had received. One morning seven converts left Banza Manteke, never more to return. They desired to go to some town about sixteen miles from the station, where the natives had always been particularly unfriendly. It was the custom for the young converts to go in this way, and at their own charges. Neither was it at all necessary for the missionary to prompt them in the matter. They felt it was not a duty but a privilege to go and preach the gospel. Though conscious that they might often imperil their lives, they went apparently without any fear. These young men were warned of their danger. Still they went joyfully, to tell the story of the cross, and of God's love to men. *They went—but they never returned.* They sealed their faith with their blood. Thus they went home to be with that Saviour whom they had so recently learned to love.

The friends and relatives of the martyred Christians came to the missionaries for comfort and advice.

"O mundele, wei tuna sa?" (O white man, what shall we do?) they tearfully asked.

"What did the disciples do when John the Baptist was beheaded?" asked the missionary. "They went and told Jesus."

Thus the brethren tried to comfort and strengthen these new and persecuted Christians.

After spending one night at Banza Manteke, we prepared to move forward toward Ntombo Lukuti. Our carriers felt otherwise. The actions of the leader of our Kru boys showed that things were ripe for desertion. Boxes and cases were brought from the storehouse and laid along the yard in order, but our men showed no disposition to take the loads assigned to them. These men had never been up the country beyond this point, and were evidently not inclined to go farther. Half of our men were Krus; the other half were Loangos. We approached the Kru headman to get him to make a move.

"Now, headman, what is the matter that we do not start?"

"We go back."

"What is the matter, that you want to go back?"

"No chop live for them road." (No food on the road.) "We no ketch plenty chop."

A little gentle persuasion convinced the obstinate headman and his carriers that there was an abundance of food in advance, and so they picked up their loads and we departed.

At noon we rested at Ntombo Lukuti, under the friendly shade of a native hut. We were thirsty after our walk, and longed for some fresh palm wine. Presently an old chief came along with a fowl to present to the white travelers. We accepted it, although we knew too well that the old gentleman was not actuated altogether by motives of pure generosity. Whenever they make a present they do it with the expectation of getting more than its value in return. There were many beautiful palm trees in and near the town, so we asked:

"Chief, we would like some 'malavu masamba.'"

"We have none, white man."

"There are many trees all around."

"But they are not mine, white man."

"Well you know the owner. Go and get us some fresh palm wine."

Expecting to get some blue beads for his trouble, the chief secured a calabash of fresh wine. This juice of the palm tree is a most refreshing drink. If drunk in a purely fresh state, it is absolutely unintoxicating. The natives, however, keep it exposed to the air and to the heat, until fermentation sets in. It is called in the Ki-kongo language, " malavu masamba." It requires knowledge to tap the palm tree, so as to get all the juice, and yet not injure the tree. Nearly everywhere there are palm trees, and one man usually makes a living by tapping the trees and collecting the juice. He may purchase the right, or receive it through his family, or from the king. If he can, he monopolizes the trade. It would be a serious offense to climb his trees and take his wine. I say *climb*, for the tree is tapped, not at its root, but at the top of the trunk, immediately below the branches. The trees are tapped at sunrise and at sunset. In the Congo palm, the juice does not flow at once, but drips from a hollow reed fixed in the tree, into a calabash placed to receive it, and tied to the tree. Three reeds and three small calabashes are fixed to each palm. The method of climbing the palm tree is interesting. The native has a hoop large enough to throw around the tree and his own body. After passing it around the tree and his loins, he hitches it together; then, with a knife in his girdle, and a large calabash suspended from his shoulder, he climbs the tree, almost horizontally, sometimes to a height of forty to fifty feet. This they do with apparent ease.

As may be expected, once in a great while they have accidents in connection with this tapping of the palm. It must be admitted that they are usually very careful, but occasionally a man who is not quite sober will unwisely seek to climb, or another will be in great haste, or a half-worn hoop may be used. In such cases the result is commonly a fall, and an injured back or broken limbs.

## CHAPTER X.

THE LUNIONZO—BAKA MBIZI—STOP THAT NOISE—SHADE AND SHELTER—PEACE AND SLEEP—HE STEPPED UPON A SHARP ROCK—HOUSE OF THE STRANGER.

A GOOD march brought us to the Lunionzo River. This was a beautiful river of very clear water, and, divesting ourselves of our clothing, we waded across and pitched our tent on the other side. Shortly after dusk, a caravan of natives passed by on their way up the country. They did not go on very far, however, but returned to the river some time during the night and greatly disturbed us. After eating our supper, which was laid on one of our boxes, we fixed our traveling beds just inside of the tent, and prepared to go to rest. Our Kru boys were lying around a small fire directly in front of our tent. The Loango boys were lying by another fire nearer to the bank of the river. At midnight, after a somewhat uneasy sleep, I was awakened by a most unearthly noise. It was a combination of cries, yells, and groans. My first impression was that a leopard had carried off one of our men, and then I thought that perhaps a crocodile had come up from the lower part of the river and seized one of our number. These and various thoughts came to me. The distressing noise continuing, I said to my fellow traveler:

"Old fellow, what is the matter?"

My friend jumped up in the bed, listened for a moment, and then exclaimed:

"There's a row among our men; between the Kru boys and the Loangos."

But there in front of us were our men, apparently wrapped in deep slumber, and unconscious of the noises that made night so hideous.

Seizing our guns, we stepped forth from the tent to the forest on the bank of the river, and shouted, "Oh, bakundi" (Oh, friends).

The noises ceased, but there was no reply.

We again concluded that one or more of our men had either been the victim of foul play, or that some dark deed was being committed in the deep shade of the forest. Again the stillness was broken by Kikongo exclamations of surprise, such as—"E-Tata! E-Mama!"

My friend and I heard these words distinctly, and both of us instantly concluded there was something radically wrong.

Again exerting all our lung power, we shouted:

"Oh, friends, what is the matter?" This, of course, in the language of the native.

There was silence for a brief moment and then a reply came from the river below us:

"Mbakanga mbizi" (I am catching fish).

"Why do you make that awful noise?"

"To get more fish."

"Well, stop that noise at once. There are white men here who want to sleep."

"Ki diambu, ko mundele" (No words, white man).

Once more we sought our tents, and, save an occasional movement of our men, who arose to rekindle the dying embers of our camp fires, or the harsh notes of some night bird, all was comfortably still.

In the morning we had a close shave with an elephant, or rather elephants, for there was a herd. While pursuing the "zinzou" (elephants) we had an adventure with buffaloes. In consequence of the high grass and the dense jungle, it was impossible to get near enough to shoot, and we were compelled, to the great disappointment of our men, to abandon the chase, and proceed on the march.

Frequently, in passing up and down the country, we found it convenient to spend a night at the Lunionzo River. The following extract from my diary will show to some extent how we traveled in the dry season :

"I am writing this under the friendly shade of some trees on the bank of the Lunionzo River. All is fixed for the night. Our men are lying down, talking over the events of the day. We are all happy, though far from the haunts of civilization, and the city's noisy din. One large tree near me, with roots above ground, and with gnarled wide-spreading branches, reminds one of the tree in the 'Village Blacksmith.' Truly it is as the shadow of a great rock in a weary land. I appreciate its shade all the more, seeing I have just been exposed to the pitiless rays of a tropical sun. One box serves for a seat; another for a table. I have no tent, neither a bed, only a camp chair and blankets. The waters of the Lunionzo looked so inviting that I treated myself to a luxurious bath. A large caravan has just arrived from Ngombe with ivory. I am lying on my chair and watching the carriers, who are engaged in burning the grass, in order to catch 'zimpuku,' or rats. At this stage of events, it would be difficult to persuade most Congo men's stomachs that rats are not intended for human food. After feasting on rats and 'kuanga' (a kind of native bread), they danced and sang most vigorously, until I thought they must be utterly weary. I am somewhat tired with my long walk, but 'even here is a season of rest,' and so, committing myself, soul and body, to him who has kept me all my life long, 'I will lay me down in peace and sleep.' The same tree that awhile ago afforded me shelter from a burning sun, will now protect me from the dews of night. Good-night."

In Congo, where there are none of the conveniences for rapid and easy transit, traveling is necessarily slow. Occasionally, a traveler may use a mule or an ox, but these are not obtainable in the country, and it is a difficult matter to get them across the many rivers. One traveler informed me, in regard to his donkey, that he was most unwilling to cross streams. So when they came to a stream or small river, a rope was tied around the donkey's neck, with the end of which a man would then swim across. Other men would next give the donkey a push, when he was looking the other way, and after a few convulsive struggles, he would usually reach the other side. I say usually, for they sometimes caused much trouble. One creature, in crossing the Luvu, managed to break the rope, and instead of reaching the other side of the river, floated down for some distance, and finally landed upon a rock in mid-stream, where he calmly surveyed his surroundings.

Traveling in a "luanda," or hammock, is all very well for a tired or sick man, but, on the whole, I would greatly prefer to walk. In fine weather the carriers will travel from twelve to twenty miles a day, and have sometimes covered over twenty-four. A tall strong carrier proves of great service in crossing streams. Where there are no canoes the streams must be forded. My plan was to divest myself of my coat, helmet, and boots; then I mounted and sat across the shoulders of a native, holding on to his head with a tenacious grasp. In this not very dignified position we struggled across, with a man on either side. On one occasion, when the water was deep and the current swift, my man stepped upon a slippery rock, and began to stagger. In vain I shouted to the man upon whose shoulders I sat, "Diata malembe" (Walk carefully). One convulsive struggle with the law of gravity, and there was a complete collapse. Of course, I was submerged and wet through and through, but I got out and walked for several hours before I could change my garments.

The arrival of a white man in a town causes great commotion, and, far into the night, the people's tongues run with great volubility. A white man does not pass through their town every day, and so all are anxious to see him and his mysterious belongings. Upon entering a town, the first thing in order is salutations. When a Ba-kongo man meets his friend, he does not shake hands, but he stands at a respectful distance, and inclining his body forward, he claps his hands several times in a peculiar manner, his friend doing the same. If he meets a superior, he may bend one knee. When a chief meets one of his subjects, if he condescends to return the salute at all, he does so by clapping the back of one hand in the palm of the other. My first attempts at salutation were altogether too clumsy for the fun-loving Congo-man. While clapping hands, various expressions are used, such as:

"Mavimpie?" (Is there health?)

"Mavimpi kuandi." (There is health.)

Or it may be: "Mbotie?" "Mboti kunandi." These terms having a similar meaning.

In the Ki-kongo language, the letter "e" sounded

as "a" in "fate," forms the interrogative. This may be placed at the end of a word in the middle of a sentence, or at the end of the same.

In most towns or villages through which we passed, we found a small hut or house set apart for the accommodation of the stranger. This hut is called the "nzo a nzenza," or house of the stranger. It is customary to give a "dash," or present to the chief, for the use of the hut, and he will not forget this. When palm wine is presented to the traveler, the chief, or some other person, will invariably take the first drink from the calabash, to show, I think, that the wine has not been poisoned. Sometimes when resting in a town at noon, I have found the natives unwilling to sell us fowls or potatoes. In that case, I would prepare to depart, and say to my men in the hearing of the town people, "I *thought* these people were kind to the white man ; but they do not want us here; come, let us go on, that we may find kind people in the next town." This is too much for them. Instantly they would go and bring a supply of food for us, with every expression of friendliness.

It is very disagreeable traveling in the rainy

season. One night, when in my tent, the wind raged furiously, the rain fell, and so did my tent, giving me a thorough drenching. Crawling from under it into the pitiless storm and darkness, I fixed a few pegs; then cuddled up in my blankets, and, like Paul in the cyclone, I "wished for the day." It is known that cords tighten when wet. This was the immediate cause of the collapse. I might have anticipated the unpleasant result, but I placed too much confidence in my man, who was at this time calmly sleeping in the " nzo a nzenza."

# CHAPTER XI.

MUKUMBUNGU—SEEKING THE UNSEEN—MY FIRST FEVER—NKE-
BANI—WAITING AT TABLE—EASILY REMEMBERED—DESERTED
—SELFISHNESS.

HAVING been on the road from Palabala for nearly one week, my friend and I were glad as we approached the Mukumbungu Mission Station.

This station is splendidly situated as regards elevation and health considerations. It is sixteen hundred feet above sea level, and commands a fine view of the great river, immediately below the Itunzima rapids.

When our missionaries first went to Mukumbungu, the people were steeped in superstition. And indeed, the majority of them are in that condition still. Very many of the younger people have embraced Christianity, but the older ones, have, for the most part, been "joined to their idols."

Among other things, they believe that the spirits of their dead go into the woods, where they continue to buy and sell and trade as usual, though unseen to mortal eye. One evening, during our three months' residence there, a man was ill in one of our towns. The "nganga" said his spirit was in a certain wood, hence his illness. At night, a crowd led by the "nganga," passed our mission on their way to the wood, to seek for the lost spirit. In such cases the "zinganga" know very well that they are deceiving the people, but they do it expecting to receive cloth for their services. In the small hours of the morning they returned, making night hideous with their noises. I was afterward told that the "nganga" claimed to have discovered the lost spirit, but in consequence of something he did not bring him back.

Previous to my going there, Mr. F. had a very painful experience. A king's brother had been sick for a long time, and no "nkisi" was able to cure him, so that the people concluded that he must be "ndoki" or bewitched. The "nganga" was brought, and a poor man was sent to eat poison. He had done so once before, and was considered as "ndoki" by the people around. This was, therefore, his second time, and if he failed this time to resist it, he would have to be killed. They can *pay* for their life the *first* time, but *not the second*. The poor condemned wretch had often heard the gospel from Mr. F., but he only appeared the more set in his course, and was now reaping the results of his own folly, and the fruits of his own worship. At first, Mr. F. questioned whether he had any right to interfere in the matter, having done all he could to *persuade* them they were wrong. But when he heard the cry of the condemned man's wife and children, as he was being taken away toward the Congo River to be drowned, he could stand it no longer, but went after him. Two men were leading the condemned by the arms, and two others walked behind with guns. Mr. F. says he shall never forget the expression on the poor man's face, as he tried again to tell him about God and the Saviour. He tried to repeat the words, but being so sick, it was with considerable difficulty. Mr. F. promised to redeem him if they would take him back, which they did after much persuasion, but it was slow work, the man was so poorly. As it was near evening, he made haste to see the king, in order to release the man, but the king had hidden himself away, and all efforts to find him were fruitless. With a heavy heart, Mr. F. left the man, in hopes of being able to do something the next day. He had not, however, left him long, when the men cut his throat, and threw his body into the river.

During my stay at Mukumbungu, I heard of many sad cases, but Mr. F. and I did not witness them, as the natives use every effort to conceal their evil deeds from the white man. In a town about an hour's journey from the mission, a woman was seized, declared to be possessed of a devil, and *cut to pieces.* The report reached us the following day. At first it was most surely believed that our missionaries stole the spirits of the natives, and sold them. Threats of personal violence, from the natives of some outlying town reached the station again and again. Into these towns Mr. F. went, speaking the truth with love and holding forth the word of life. He was never molested, the God of Daniel being with him. He carried no weapon, only a stick, but the angel of the Lord was near him. Often have I seen him, seated on some fallen palm tree, surrounded by forty or fifty heathens, and heard him speak " mambu ma moyo," or words of life. The seed thus sown has already brought forth fruit.

While at this station I contracted my first fever; how I do not know. Some persons who have never seen Congo suppose these fevers are caused by swamps. Let me say that you may travel for days in Congo, and not see a swamp of any size. Others suppose that they are caused by the effluvium from the decaying vegetation, while others again suppose that the heat in Congo is very intense. The vegetation has probably something to do with it. As to the heat, ordinarily it was not uncomfortably warm, and yet exposure to the sun is invariably followed by ill effects. As the result of my own experience, I would say that exposure and fatigue are two prime causes of fever in Congo.

While at this station we ransomed a little girl named Nkebani. It cost us less than fifteen dollars to do this. When she was brought to us and offered for *sale*, she was in a very unclean condition. Poor little girl! how little did she realize that this transaction between the white man and her master would be the turning point in her life! After a good deal of talk, the necessary number of "minlele," or clothes, were handed to her master, and Nkebani was *free*. We at once put her to assist our boys in cleaning our rooms, and laying the table, etc. Evidently Nkebani thought we were unnecessarily particular about the arrangement of things on the table, and the kind of food we ate. The first time we got her to wait at the table, she came in and promptly squatted on the floor. We said:

"Nkebani, stand up."

She obeyed, but at once leaned against the wall.

"Nkebani, stand here by the table."

She came forward, and leaned half across the table.

"Nkebani, don't lie on the table in that way; stand up so."

She promptly responded, but at first I think she regarded it as a kind of punishment. At home (?) she had been quite at liberty to lie on the floor, and to roll in the dust, if she felt inclined; why should the white man place these restrictions upon her movements?

But she was anxious to please, and to make herself generally useful. The relative uses of the food and condiments on the table sorely puzzled Nkebani. Toward the close of our meal she would frequently offer the mustard or vinegar to us. Then it appeared easier to *push* things around the table than to *carry* them; so instruction was necessary.

"Nkebani, don't *push* things; *carry* them."

To all these instructions the little girl paid attention; and to-day Nkebani, who is at Palabala Station, is making satisfactory progress.

The names of our mission boys at Mukumbungu, and of others who lived near the station and attended school, will be interesting to my readers. They are as follows: Lulebako, Kondi, Wili, Jese, Bayunga, Sitakodila, Lubiandu, Makumgisa, Matewanga, Mpebolo, Kindeli, Baku, Mapingani, Nzuzi, Teka, Mazela, Bafuka, Mayola, Nkoba, Nkomo, Ngumba, Maboza, Ngoma. Many of these have been baptized on confession of their faith in the Lord Jesus.

One evening, about sunset, as I was seated outside in the veranda, three men called. Each of them carried a small bundle, and a supply of native food. The whole of the face of one of them was tatooed in a wonderful manner. This was the spokesman. Advancing to where I sat, he bowed and begged to be permitted to stay all night in the Loangos' quarters. He spoke English fairly well. On inquiry, I found they were from the Island of Fernando Po. They had engaged to go to Stanley Pool, tò work for the English Baptist Mission. The tatooed man said that one of their number had been taken sick one week before, and had just died one day behind. His story appeared straightforward, and we believed it. Of course, we made inquiries.

"How long since you came to Banana?"

"Two weeks and half a week."

"What time did you start from Tundua?"

"Two weeks pass."

"Well, where have you been on the road so long?"

"This man he take sick one week pass."

"Did you take care of him?"

"Yes, masta, we do our best."

"Where is the sick man now?"

"He die, masta."

"When did he die?"

"One day pass, when the sun was there" (pointing).

"And you are sure you buried him?"

"Yes, masta."

There was every evidence of sincerity and truthfulness in their replies, so we thought no more of them, when they departed on the morrow.

Five days after this, Mr. F. went for a missionary tour in the direction of Banza Manteke. Returning in the evening, and when about a mile and a half from the station, he was informed by some natives that there was a sick man near the roadside. With the aid of the natives he found the man in a ditch, entirely naked, and in a dying state.

Leaving his man by him, Mr. F. hurried home for my hammock, to carry the poor fellow to our place. Our men brought him to the station, and we placed him in the house of the Loangos. He was unable to speak, and notwithstanding all our efforts he died in about eighteen hours. He was horribly emaciated, having lived at least six days and six nights without any food. Having nothing to pay the natives, they of course refused him any assistance. They did not even come and tell us, so utterly selfish are these dark souls. The poor fellow was undoubtedly taken ill on the road and deserted by his companions, after they had stripped him of the few things he possessed.

The morning after he died, our Loango men buried him near the mission, in a spot we selected for a burying ground. As we stood around the open grave, with all our boys and men, I looked into it where the body lay, covered only by a blanket and a "twanda" mat, and I thought: "This is the first grave; whose will be the next?"

# CHAPTER XII.

HUNTING—ZINZOU ZAZINGI—FACE TO FACE—STILL IN DEATH—
A DELICATE MORSEL.

YEARS ago, when we went to school, little was known of Central Africa. We had some knowledge of the countries of the coast, but the great interior was as a sealed book. From Cape Bon in the north to Cape of Good Hope in the south, from Cape Guardafui in the east to Cape Verde in the west, it was, for the most part, "The Dark Continent." Our maps of Africa were marked "Unexplored Interior," "Great Desert," etc. This was particularly the case in regard to the Congo country. Captain Tuckey in 1816 sailed up the river for about one hundred and ten miles. Coming to the Yelala Falls, he could proceed no farther. Of the vast regions beyond that, nothing definite was known until, in 1877, the great explorer, Henry M. Stanley, came down the Congo, having crossed the continent from Zanzibar. New explorers and missionaries have penetrated into the interior, and have discovered fruitful countries, inhabited by numerous tribes and teeming with animal life. In some regions countless herds of elephants and buffaloes roam over its vast plains, or wade along the banks of its mighty rivers, while in the deep shade of the jungle is the home of the leopard. In other parts the king of the forest and rhinoceros are monarchs of all they survey. In its waters are found the ponderous hippopotamus and the crocodile, with its hard, scaly hide.

Hunting the elephant and buffalo is attended with considerable peril, and much judgment and caution is necessary in order to approach them with reasonable safety. Here the services of a native are invaluable. He knows their haunts; he is familiar with their modes of defense; he can tell when they are angry and about to charge; he will enter the jungle, with cat-like step, and discover their position. In these respects the African is superior to the most intelligent white man.

During our residence in the Congo country, we had several adventures with buffaloes and elephants. Not that we ever made a point of hunting, as our time was too precious; but there were times when we could win the friendship of the natives by going to their help; and this was something not to be lost sight of.

One afternoon, while at Mukumbungu Station, some natives ran up excitedly, and said:

"Oh, mundele, zinzou zazingi; zina muna mavia metu."

In English that would mean: "Oh, white man, there are many elephants in our fields."

"When did you see them?"

"This morning, 'nsuka, nsuka'" (early, early).

"Are there any male elephants?"

"Yes, white man, there are."

"Can you not shoot them with your guns?"

"No, white man; our guns are not as good as yours."

"Well, see here; because we are your friends, we will come to help you in the morning."

"Mabiza, mundele" (Good, white man).

We prepared to start early next morning. Mr. F. and myself, well equipped, and attended by two men and our boys, to carry our water bottles, umbrellas, and guns, started two hours before daylight, so as to find the elephants before they retired into the forest for the forenoon. After a pretty hard walk of ten miles, through tall grass, tangled creepers, and brushwood, our men became cautious, and presently one of them exclaimed :

"Nguilu e nzou" (I hear an elephant).

There was no mistaking that sound—urmph, urmph, urmph. With guns cocked, we followed our guide to the edge of the forest. There, right before us, was a huge male elephant, with massive tusks. We shall not soon forget our feelings at that moment. Taking aim as well as the trees would permit, we both fired and the monster fell. Rising instantly, it plunged through the forest in the direction of the Kuilu River. Though we followed as fast as possible, we could not overtake it. Outside the forest the whole herd appeared, fully thirty in all, and all making for the river. It is a noted fact, that whenever elephants are attacked, they will at once make for the nearest river, evidently to get rid of their pursuers. The large male which was wounded kept in the rear, between us and the other elephants. The chase grew exciting. The sun was fearfully hot, and we were out of breath.

Two more shots were fired, and a female elephant fell. Reaching the top of a ridge near the river, we were compelled to take a brief rest, while our men continued the pursuit. Down on the plain by the river, our men made a brave and last attack upon the herd before they swam across. Again and again the large male turned upon our men with uplifted trunk, and each time he met the deadly bullet. It was an exciting scene. Into the river the whole herd plunged, and swam to the other side. Not all, however, for the wounded female died midstream, and began to float down. The male reached the other side, but was so severely wounded, that he died from loss of blood. He was afterward found "tremendous still in death." We were anxious to get the ears and tusks of the female, while our men were equally anxious to get "zimbizi zazingi," or plenty of meat. But we felt the risk was too great, so we persuaded them to abandon the carcass. We called their attention to a crocodile, and warned the men to keep out of the river. The temptation was too strong, and two stalwart natives plunged into the water, shouting the meanwhile, to frighten the crocodiles. It was an anxious moment for us all, as we kept our guns pointed at the river, in case a crocodile appeared. We had seen a large one, fully twelve feet long, higher up the river, but happily he remained there. Our men, who were greatly excited, towed the dead elephant to the bank.

The natives were thankful to us for saving their crops, and for furnishing them with plenty of meat. It was now dark, and we were many miles from our station. We trudged along as well as we could through the darkness. Our house was built of clay walls and grass roof, and could not boast of windows; yet how cheerful it seemed on our return that night, for it was our home! Our people met us with shouts of joy, and, to convince them that we had been successful, we showed the trunk, which had been carried home upon the shoulders of our men, and which is considered by the Congo people as the most delicate part of the elephant.

# CHAPTER XIII.

LUKUNGU—ELEPHANTS AND CROCODILES—THE SWING BRIDGE—LOST HIS BALANCE—GYMNAST.

LUKUNGU station is about two hundred and thirty miles from Banana, and was established in 1882. The mission buildings are close to the river called the Lukungu, which is from twenty to forty yards wide. The Congo Free State authorities have a station one mile from the mission. This station was formerly occupied by Mr. and Mrs. Ingham. Mr. Ingham has slain many a lordly elephant which came too near his deadly rifle. The fact that he has actually killed "zinzou zazingi" (many elephants) has raised him very high in the estimation of the natives. In the Lukungu River crocodiles are found, and are sometimes quite troublesome. Once, when Mr. Ingham was there, a crocodile came out of the river for several nights, and tried to get the pigs. He was thinking of sending to Banza Manteke for a tiger trap, when one of the little boys came running and told him that he could see it. Mr. Ingham shot it under the strong plate which protects the ear; and all hands being unable to drag it out of the river, they towed it around to a little stream, and tied it up for the night, the Kru boys looking forward to "plenty beef" on the morrow.

The next day it was skinned and cut open. In its stomach was found a portion of a pig, one hundred and five stones, two copper anklets, of native make, such as women wear, and two red beads. The anklets and beads were afterward identified as belonging to a woman named "Vanga Mbote." The crocodile was fifteen feet in length, and four feet nine inches and a half round the body. The natives were horrified at the sight of the anklets, and the Kru boys would not eat any of the meat.

As it was often necessary to cross the river to reach the market, and Mayambula, and other towns, the brethren built a bridge. Some of my readers would not want to cross such a "kiamvu," or bridge. Nearly opposite the station are several large trees, with their branches reaching far over the water. By the aid of creepers from the forest, twined together in a sort of network, a swing bridge was formed. This was secured to the trees on one side, and stretched across to those on the opposite side, at an elevation of about twenty feet. It was shaky, and gave one the impression of walking on air, but it was tolerably safe. We have seen more than one creep over it in a horizontal position, not daring to stand up. It was like taking exercise on a tight rope, or rather a slack rope. Natives seldom ventured over it with loads, but went across the ford. One native who did attempt it came to grief. I was standing near the bridge at the time. Our friend had three little barrels of gunpowder, tied together with palm branches, carrying upon his head. Mounting the approach to the bridge, he ventured to cross, and did reach the centre of the bridge, where he lost his equilibrium, and after a short but severe struggle, he went down, twenty feet into the river. Like a cork he rose, still grasping his kegs of powder, and struggled to the side, and then crossed by the ford. I was really sorry for our poor friend, and inquired if he were hurt, though the temptation to laugh was irresistible. The manner in which he seized those kegs, and struck off across the shallow water, clearly showed that no bones were broken.

One day as I was about to mount the bridge, I disturbed a sleeping crocodile, and, with a sudden start, he plunged into the water. Our little boys had often bathed in that same pool. A monkey of a large species used to come to the trees around our bridge. For what purpose I cannot say. His gymnastic powers were simply marvelous. How lightly he vaulted from branch to branch; from tree to tree; from side to side! They are fond of peanuts, and often make a raid on the natives' peanut gardens. The natives, too, are fond of monkey, and sometimes capture one who has fattened on their peanuts. Snakes are occasionally met with. One day when seated in our mission house, a snake coiled around the ridge-pole, looked down, and surveyed his surroundings. Seizing my gun, I fired through the roof, and shot the creature through the middle, and found his length nearly six feet. One day my boy "Kivwila" found a little lizard under my pillow, while making my bed. It measured four and a half inches, and its bite is poisonous.

During the hottest weather, I left the shutters of my bedroom windows open. There was no glass, and one night, about 11 P. M., some animal probably a bush cat, jumped through a window, near my bed, and after upsetting the crockery, sprang through the opposite window.

Early one morning I was called to see a man who had been shot. He lived in the town of Mayambula. In another town a man had been taken sick, and this native of Mayambula was declared to be the cause. The sick man's friends, with an "nganga," came and demanded him who caused the sickness. They would not give him up. That night, under cover of the darkness, a friend of the sick man came stealthily to the town of Mayambula and shot the innocent victim. I found him lying on his side, and groaning piteously. On his hip was a gaping wound, where the slugs had penetrated. I could not extract them, nor could anything be done, save to relieve the pain. In the evening, after I left, an "nganga" foolishly tried to probe the wound and extract the slugs, but of course, without any effect It only hastened his death, which took place that night.

Life and Scenes in Congo. STANLEY POOL, OR LEOPOLDVILLE. Page 133.

# CHAPTER XIV.

PAYING THE CARRIERS—DIFFICULT TO SATISFY—REJOICING IN HIS RICHES—CONQUERED AT LAST.

MY readers are aware that there is a Cataract region in Congo. For a distance of two hundred and thirty miles the river is not navigable, owing to a series of cataracts and rapids. The first is the Yelala Falls, one hundred and fifteen miles from the mouth of the river; then there are other falls and rapids, about thirty-two in all, extending to Leopoldville, or Stanley Pool. The "Henry Reed," the missionary steamer, was carried overland this entire distance, on the heads of native and other carriers.

All requisites for up country stations have to be conveyed in this manner, though the same caravans do not carry them the entire distance. One caravan may carry the goods from Tundua to Palabala; then another will carry them forward to Lukungu; while a third will carry them to the Pool. It is common to speak of Leopoldville as the Pool. It is also known as Kintamo, and has yet another name, Mpumbulu. How many more I cannot say. If possible, each of the loads is limited to sixty-four pounds gross. It is not easy to persuade a native to carry a heavier load than that, though he may do so for an extra consideration. When carrying on his own account, a native will frequently struggle along under a burden of one hundred and twenty pounds. But the missionary should not and does not expect it. The native, too, is particular as to the nature, the shape, the size, and the bulk of his load. A coil of brass wire may weigh seventy pounds, while a large tin trunk, with clothing, may be under sixty. The native will usually prefer the coil of wire, because of its smallness and compactness and because it may be handled a little more roughly. Another reason is that, owing to the tall grass sometimes overhanging the road like an arch, it is difficult to make satisfactory progress with a bulky article on the head. Sometimes, too, a native is apt to judge the weight of an article according to its size. The missionary or other traveler will deal with these little difficulties as best he can.

As yet there is no currency in the country. Fowls,

sheep, goats, fish, potatoes, "kuanga," fruits, and other things have to be purchased; carriers and other workmen have to be paid. Money is of little value to the native, having no purchasing power. If he received it, it would only be to use it for ornamental purposes. It cannot be used for the necessaries of life, nor exchanged for the ivory of the interior. There is a currency, but it varies in different parts. It may be "nganata" beads at Palabala; blue beads at Lukungu and brass rods at the Pool or the Equator. Hence it will be seen that it costs something to take our money or currency up country. Carriers do not demand payment in currency. They will take cloth or handkerchiefs. They also get beads or knives to purchase food while traveling.

Hunting up men, arranging as to the pay, marshaling them in order, giving out and receiving loads, and paying the carriers, takes up a good deal of the time and taxes the patience of the missionary. One who has had any experience with these caravans will be careful to select the strongest men, and to give out the heaviest loads first. If he distributes the lighter loads first, the heavy ones will probably be left behind.

An unwilling, lazy, or troublesome carrier may be chaffed, coaxed, encouraged, warned or even threatened with advantage.

Starting a caravan is an exciting time. Disputes with each other, and high words, are the order of the day. Each man has something important to say, and must have a hearing. The "kapita," or leader of the caravan, has his hands full, and indeed frequently requires the assistance of the missionary. Some "kapitas" have the necessary qualities of a leader, and the men are quick to perceive this. All being ready for the march, we give the signal of command, "Tu kuenda kuetu" (we go), and away we start. Once the men are fairly under way, there is little more trouble.

The arrival of a caravan causes more excitement than the departure of one, because the carriers have not only to deposit their loads, but also to receive their pay. This to them is an all-important event. The loads are received, checked, and examined, then the carriers will receive so many pieces of cloth, according to agreement. They crowd around the little door of the store, each one speaking vociferously. These "minlele," or cloths, are really common prints, and worth about fifty cents each. One piece is equal in size to about twelve handkerchiefs, the prints being usually bright colored and attractive in appearance. The carrier may use a portion of his cloth to wear around his loins, or he may store it up so as to purchase a wife or a slave, or he may use it to trade in the markets. They are very particular as to the design and color of the print. Some prints cause quite a boom, and become popular in the district for a time. Others, quite as good, may lie for a long time in the store, before they can be disposed of. It is a mistake to suppose that anything will attract the attention of the Congo native, or that they may be easily imposed upon. They will examine the cloth with the air of a "connoisseur," measure its width, determine its quality, ascertain its length, and see if it has printed colors on both sides.

The missionary has the names of the carriers on the manifest or way-bill. These names he calls, the calls being repeated vigorously by the men—" Ndunga, Kalandenga, Mayengisa." Each man responds to his name.

" Here is your pay."

"I don't want that, white man; I want that other cloth you used to give."

"That is all gone; you must take this."

"You don't give enough, white man."

"I give you all I promised on your 'nkanda'" (book).

"Give me one handkerchief or a knife?"

"No, this is your pay; will you take it?"

"Ah, no, white man; I won't."

"You won't take it? Well, next man—Kalandenga, come on."

"These cloths are not long enough."

"Yes, they are the right length. See, I will measure it."

"I want 'malensua'" (handkerchiefs).

"Well, here they are."

"That color is not good, white man."

"Won't you take this cloth or these handkerchiefs?"

"Ve, mundele; ka mbote ko" (No, white man; they are not good).

"Well, if you do not like these things, go away now, and come again. I must go, and can not wait any longer. See, I lock the door, and go to our school."

The missionary then goes into the house, while the carriers will hold a prolonged discussion in the yard. Gradually their excitement abates, and they depute one of their number—generally the "kapita"—to tell the missionary that they will accept his terms.

"Mundele."

"Well, what is it?"

"The men will take the cloth."

"Will they take the quantity they agreed upon?"

"Yes, 'ki diambu ko'" (no palaver—literally, no word).

And each man departs, rejoicing in his riches.

# CHAPTER XV.

MAVUZI'S LETTER—KIVUILA'S LETTER—MARKETS IN CONGO—
IN THE MARKET—THE SITE OF THE MARKET—THINGS FOR
SALE—TEMPTING MORSELS—THEFT IN THE MARKET—AWFUL
PUNISHMENT.

WHILE staying at Lukungu, I asked some of our boys to write a letter or two, that I might present them to my friends in America. They thought it was a good idea, and so commenced the great undertaking of writing a letter, or rather letters. The boy Mavuzi was able to write in English. Here is a copy of his letter.

LUKUNGU STATION MISSION.
August the 29th (1886).

My dear friends: I hope you are all quit well as we are in present of God.

I am very glad to see that God is sending some more missions (missionaries) to tell us the love of Jesus Christ.

I wish you will come out in Congo to tell thous (those) wich have not heard the wonderful story of Jesus and his love, and I am learning more about Jesus so that I may tell my own people about Jesus. There are plenty souls lost here. Let us thank God because he have send his Holy Spirit at Mbanza Manteke and I am very glad because a sister of mine she is saved.

Let us think what Jesus said when he was in the world. And he said unto them go ye into all the world and preach the gospel to every creature.

Mission (missionary) which has been with me tells me about Christian young men in America. I send my love to them all.

I remain your friend in Jesus,

FREDERICK MEYER MAVUZI.
*Congo boy.*

When Mavuzi presented his letter, I said "Thank you, Mavuzi. I will show it to many friends in America." This appeared to please him. There was one boy at the station of whom I was very fond. His name was Kivuila. He scarcely spoke any English, so I desired him to attempt a letter in the Kikongo language. He readily consented, and after several hours, produced the following, a few words of which we give as he wrote it:

LUKUNGU STATION.

Engua bakundi bami Nzambi diadi kiavesila emindele miayiza kutulongi. Tutondele kuetu beni. Wau yetu tukilonganga nkonta a Jesus, kansi wantu kabanzaidi nkonta a Jesus ko.

The following is a free translation of it:

"Dear friends of mine, God that send white men to come us teach, we thank we much. Now we learning about Jesus. But people no they know about Jesus no. People they kill one another only. I working in house mission or season (year) three or four. We reading book about words of God. White men of us teaching words of wonder of Jesus. People they will not believe Jesus and they will not believe words of his. Sister of mine staying across the water, and brothers also and mother of mine dead seasons of many."

Some of the writer's words are unintelligible and hence are by no means easy to decipher and translate.

In the Lukungu district there are several markets. These as well as the other markets of Congo are full of interest to the traveler as well as to the aborigines of the country. Here the missionary or explorer has an opportunity to replenish his supply of food. There is, of course, a wide difference between the markets of Congo and the bazaars of Eastern lands, and great changes must evidently take place before our missionaries can present the gospel at these markets with any degree of success. At other times and places, they will usually listen respectfully to the "mambu ma nzenza," or strange words of the missionary, but during the few hours they are at the market, they are so taken up with buying, selling, and looking on, that the missionary cannot command their attention. I do not blame them for this. It is desirable to speak to them in crowds. The time may come when the market will afford better opportunities. At the beginning of the market, they are busily engaged fixing their wares; those that remain to the close are usually loafers, half muddled with stale palm wine, from some calabash, and in anything but a fit condition to listen to the words of life. I say I am not blaming them for being interested in buying and selling. It would not be easy to win the attention of people in any one of our own markets. It would hardly be considered wise to attempt it. Still, the missionary in Congo rarely misses an opportunity to sow the seed of the kingdom—in the native town, by the wayside, at the mission station, nor even at the market.

There are four days in the Congo week. Here they are: "Konzo," "Nkenge," "Nsona," Nkandu." On each of these days a market is held somewhere. Local markets are commonly called by the day on which they are held. A love of trading is characteristic of the African, though by no means confined to that race. If a Congo man has a pig to sell, and a purchaser is at hand to-day, the owner will wait until the morrow, and sell it at the market. Even the little children love to buy and sell. Each person loves to feel that he has an active interest in the affairs of life. As Mrs. H. G. Guinness says: "The market, to the natives of Africa, seems to be what the Royal Exchange is to the merchants of London, the universal and important rendezvous." Stanley graphically describes the African markets:

"These markets on the banks of the Congo, at intervals of three or four miles, are central resorts of the aborigines from either bank, and considered as neutral ground, which no chief may claim, nor any individual assert claims of tribute for.

"Many of them are wide grassy spaces under the shade of mighty spreading trees, affording admirable river scenes for an artist.

"In the background is the deep black forest, apparently impenetrable in its density; here and there a taller giant, having released itself from acquaintance and familiarity, overlooks its neighbors;

its branches are favored by the white-collared eagle and the screaming ibis. Here and there rise the feathery and graceful fronds of the elæis palm. In the foreground flows the broad, brown river. In the morning, on market days, the grassy plots are thronged. From the depths of the forest, and from isolated clearings, from lonely islands, and from the open country of the "Bakusu," come together the aborigines with their baskets of "cassava," their mats of palm fibre and sedge, their gourds of palm wine, their beans and maize, millet and sugar cane, crockery, and the handiwork of their artisans in copper and iron and wood, the vermilion camwood, their vegetables, and fruit of banana and plantain, their tobacco and pipes and bangles, their fish nets and baskets, fish, and a multitude of things which their wants and tastes have taught them to produce.

"All is animation and eager chatter until noon, when the place becomes silent again and untenanted, a prey to gloom and shade, where the hawk and the eagle, the ibis, the grey parrot, and the monkey may fly, and scream, and howl undisturbed."

The money or currency is brass rods, "cowries"

(small shells), blue beads, white beads, and formerly iron wire. In the Congo market, rats find a ready sale. Often have we seen the vendor of rats taking his place in the busy throng with his commodity, which the native is very expert in catching. With a small basket trap of his own construction, he will disturb the rats by beating or burning the tall grass, and will invariably secure his prize. After he has captured a number, he will singe the hair off and fix them on rods—say ten on each rod. In this condition he offers the tempting morsels for sale.

The butcher of the market is an object of interest. He drives his pig to market, and kills it just outside the circle of trade. He cooks it, also, partially. As a sign of his calling, the butcher takes a piece of fat, and secures it to the top of his head by means of a skewer. The natives sometimes get very excited in trading, and can hardly control themselves. Under the influence of palm wine, guns and other weapons would be dangerous instruments in their hands, and they are conscious of this. Because of this, for their own safety, they have a law which forbids any one to carry a gun within the limits of the market. All who bring weapons must hide them in the grass outside the market place, and any one who violates this law, endangers his own life. Although the punishment for stealing at the market is so terribly severe, yet instances of theft are by no means of rare occurrence. A thief may possibly escape with his life the first time, if he has friends who can pacify the injured parties; but for the second offense there is no escape, be he chief or slave. This is not because of their admiration for the negative commandment, known to us as the eighth in the decalogue, but because they find it absolutely necessary, in order to make their markets a success; or, at least, they appear to think that these severe laws are necessary. Apart from that, honesty, be it remembered, is not a predominating virtue in a Congo native. When a thief is captured, he is speedily condemned to die, and that sentence is quickly carried into effect.

I stood in the centre of a large market, with a native, looking sadly at the many graves.

"Are all these mounds graves?" I asked.

"Yes, white man, 'minkala mia yevi'" (graves of thieves).

"Thieves!—why, what did they steal?"

"They came to the 'zandu' (market), and they were caught stealing."

"But do you put to death those that steal in the market?"

"Kedika, mundele" (Truth, white man).

"Tell me how."

"Sometimes they shoot them; or they may strangle them, or kill them with the knife; or they may put them into a hut, fill it with grass, and then burn them alive."

"What is that sticking up through the top of the grave?"

"It is a piece of a gun. That man would bring his 'nkeli' (gun) into the market; so they killed him, buried his body in that hole, and stuck his gun through his body."

With a sickening sensation I turned away from the mound-like graves and the protruding gun stocks.

The noise and excitement at a Congo market is very great. The Makwekwe market is frequently attended by from five hundred to one thousand people.

Two hours in such a market is sufficient to bring on a splitting headache. Stanley says:

"How like any other market place it was, with its noise and murmur of human voices. The same rivalry in extolling their wares, the eager, quick motion, the emphatic gesture, the inquisitive look, the facial expressions of scorn and triumph, anxiety, joy, plausibility were all there."

Oh, that they were as anxious to hear and receive the gospel, as they are to buy and sell and get gain!

# CHAPTER XVI.

STANLEY POOL—THE BATEKE—LEOPOLDVILLE—UPPER CONGO TRADERS—ON BOARD THE HENRY REED—THE BEAUTIES OF THE POOL—NO KETCH BOTTOM—A FROG CONCERT—THE EN AVANT—EXTENDED JAWS—A NARROW ESCAPE—CLOCK POINT —SEIZED BY A CROCODILE—U-P-R-A-A—BOLOBO—BOLOBO NATIVES—LET GO THAT FISH—MALAMU BAA—MODE OF EXECUTION—A WEIRD SCENE—NYAMA BAA—WA-T-CH—COLLARS NOT OF LINEN—KILLED BY A BUFFALO.

IMMEDIATELY after leaving Lukungu, the character of the people alters very perceptibly. The chiefs appear to be more important; the towns are larger, and the buildings somewhat more substantial; domestic slavery is carried on to a greater extent, and the native market becomes a centre of great interest. In the line of travel between Lukungu and Stanley Pool, there is a very important market, called the Makwekwe market. This is a central meeting place for the busy native traders.

After crossing the deep and swift Nkisi River, the people are known as "Ba-ntandu," which may be translated as Highlanders. Hitherto, they have not proved themselves to be a very enterprising people. The frequent passing of travelers up and down the country has had a beneficial effect upon them, and they are becoming somewhat more industrious, and more disposed to welcome the traveler and missionary. About two days from Stanley Pool, we first came in contact with the Ba-wumbu tribe. These people are, to some extent, in the ivory trade with the Bateke people, who live beyond. Their chief interest, however, is in their immense mandioca fields, their fowls, and their goats. They are of a rather better disposition than the Bantandu people, and usually give a welcome to the passing traveler. Of the Bateke people who live around Stanley Pool, or Leopoldville, Dr. Sims very properly says:

"They are great thieves, and difficult to barter with; they like to buy cheap and sell dear; are extremely exorbitant in their demands, are impertinent, rude, and brusque. The chiefs wear plenty of cloth, trailing it on the ground in pretentious fashion,; clean, as regards the skin, but never washing their garments, thinking highly of them when colored with red sandal wood, dye, and dirt. The coiffure is exceedingly well done as a chignon, a brass or iron hairpin projecting from it.

"Red, yellow, and white clay is sometimes used to put a square around an eye, sometimes to draw a diagonal line from ear to chin, down the forehead and nose, or across the eyelids and nose. Streaks are also run down the abdomen and down the arms."

The Bateke at Kintamo are largely engaged in commercial pursuits—that is, they are great traders in slaves and ivory. Each Bateke chief prides himself in the number of his slaves, who together with his wives and children, form a numerous household. As a tribe, the Bateke do not till the soil. They are traders rather than agriculturists. From the Bayanzi, who live beyond them, they buy fish and fermented liquors, and from the Bambuno, they obtain fowls, goats, peanuts, and "kwanga."

The natives who live on the banks of the upper Congo make long voyages for trading purposes. This they do in canoes. It is an interesting sight to see several large trading canoes, each containing thirty to thirty-eight people, and a large quantity of barter goods, passing up the river, working their paddles to a monotonous chant, and keeping near the shore, so as to have the benefit of the back current. These traders often travel by night. When they do so, they chant most vigorously, and blow several huge ivory horns, to signfy to the natives in the towns along the banks, that they have peaceable (?) intentions. Right well do I remember being roused from my sleep, to stand and gaze at these peace-loving traders, our dwelling at that time being right on the south bank of the Congo, and about eight hundred miles from the coast. A boy or man stands at the prow of the canoe, holding aloft a flaming torch, made from gum-copal. The effect on a clear dark night is very striking.

Stanley Pool is difficult to navigate on account of the numerous sandbanks. In some places, however, it is very deep. Large numbers of hippopotami and crocodiles sport in these waters, but it is not easy to capture them. Much of the land around Stanley Pool is thickly wooded, and, in these woods, with their dense brushwood, and tangled creepers and tall grass, snakes are sometimes found. One large snake fully eight feet in length came and took our fowls.

This was repeated again and again. Before we could get our gun, he disappeared in the long grass, and to look for him would have been madness. One of our mission men, however, ultimately shot a large specimen, as he was trying to gorge a fowl which he had seized.

There are several small steamers at Stanley Pool, including the American Baptist Mission Steamer, the "Henry Reed." On this pretty little craft we made a voyage to our Equator Station, about four hundred and fifty miles. It gave us an oportunity of seeing more of the beauties of the Pool, and also something of the natives who live along the river's banks. On board we had Mr. B., the engineer; Mr. W., of the English Baptist Mission; and Capt. Masari, an Italian explorer, who was going up the Mobanga River. We had also twelve natives and Loangos; six Zanzibaris and six boys. These were employed as woodchoppers, firemen, cook, washerman, throwing the lead, and other duties. Our steamer was heavily laden. We had also a whale boat with us, filled with an extra supply of firewood.

The departure of the steamer from Stanley Pool

Life and Scenes in Congo.

THE "HENRY REED."

Page 154.

for the great interior is always an interesting event. Will anything happen? Will she ever return? Will she come to grief on rocks or sandbanks? Will she fall into the hands of treacherous natives? Who can tell? All was ready. Mr. G., Baron von Nymptsh and others go on shore. The ropes are cast off; the signal is given; we swing around. The white men on shore, and a crowd of wondering natives, give us a cheer, to which we all respond right heartily, and away we go, our objective point being eight hundred miles from the coast. As we moved away from the last trace of civilization, my prayer was, "May we be kept from rocks and storms and evil men; may we get to the desired haven." I cannot, in a few words, describe the varied beauties of Stanley Pool. It is about two hundred and fifty square miles in extent. In the centre there is a large island, inhabited by elephants, buffalo, and other animals. These creatures swim to and from the mainland with ease. Stanley Pool has some seventeen islands, the largest of which is thirteen miles in length. "Innumerable water birds," says a writer, "storks, pelicans, cormorants, herons, egrets, sacred ibises, spur-winged and

Egyptian geese, terns and plovers, frequent the thick tangles of the high grass, and the many sandbanks." Look at the hippo, fifty yards away; and there's another, and another. They must weigh several tons each. What mouths! What big heads! I would like to put a few bullets into the head of one of them, so that our men might rejoice over his flesh. With a dash and a plunge, they descend into the depths, leaving the disturbed water to tell where they have gone down. And look—just beyond, there are crocodiles, submerged in the water, or on the sandbank, basking in the sun We are interested in them, but what must they think of us? We have hitherto been the lords of these waters, but now there are big things around us and floating over our heads, and defying even us.

The strong waters of Kalina Point are passed in safety. This point takes its name from Lieutenant Kalina, a member of the Congo Free State, who was drowned while attempting to pass the river in a canoe.

The French station "Mfwa" on the north bank is now sighted, and we make for the north side of the long island. The weather was lovely, and of course we were a happy party on board, and had an enjoyable time.

Dover Cliffs, on the northwest of the Pool, are really grand. They are formed of white sandstone; and as you approach them, you are reminded of some great cathedral. Their summits crowned with soft, green grass, their white walls reflecting the morning's sunlight, make a very fine picture. It is best seen at a distance, however, as, if you attempt to run on the shore, and step on the bank, you find to your dismay that you are on and in a large bed of quicksand. The current is rapid on the whole, and it took us seven and a half hours steaming to get out of the Pool. The sandbanks were at this time hidden by about two feet of water, so that it made navigation somewhat difficult. We kept a man constantly occupied in throwing out the lead. His sonorous voice would be heard after each heave of the lead: "And a half two." "By de mark fo'." "By de mark tree." "N-o ketch bottom."

We yerily sailed into the dusk of evening, as it was nearly dark when we dropped anchor for the night. Anchoring for the night is an important matter on this river, as a storm may come on, and cause the anchor to drag, or a floating island may strike the steamer. Hence it is desirable to lie close to the shore, if the trees do not prevent it. We had sufficient accommodation in our little cabin for five or six to sleep; but Mr. W. and myself preferred to sleep outside, on the top of the cabin. There was an awning over the whole steamer, and we fixed curtains on the sides, so that on the whole we were quite comfortable.

The "Enzo nzimbu"—otherwise the mosquito bar—is indispensable, if one would rest. Nor will he rest with it, unless somewhat insensible to the noises that assail him. Among the creators of these, the frogs easily hold the supremacy. There seemed a whole host of them, and suggested to me that one of the plagues of Egypt had repeated itself. But despite the concourse of sounds, far from sweet, we slept, and slept soundly.

We rose at five-thirty, steamed away at six, and in three hours we passed the spot where the "En Avant" struck on a rock on the 1st of October, 1885. The few passengers and crew managed to get to some trees on the bank, in time to save themselves. The little steamer was repaired some time afterward, and did more service on the great river.

The scenery in the narrow gorge beyond Stanley Pool is surpassingly grand. In this region the river varies in width from one to four miles, while the high hills on either side are mostly well wooded, down to the water's edge. The trees that line the banks, while reflecting their dark-green hues in the waters, afford a grateful shade from an afternoon's sun. As a writer remarks: "During the dry season a strong wind from the sea draws up this narrow gully with great force; and being against the strong current, turns the Congo into a nasty 'choppy' sea." This makes it difficult to tow boats alongside. Canoes travel in these waters, but because of the roughness, frequently have to lay to and wait, or travel in the night. It is a common sight to see the traders in camp on the banks of the Upper Congo, unable to steer their heavily laden canoes on the stormy waters. There are many rocks about this part of the river, and this did not tend to tranquilize one's feelings. Hippopotami and crocodiles are sufficiently numerous to assure one that there would be little chance of escape, if anything happened to the steamer. What capacious jaws these crocodiles had! Some of our missionaries were once taking a row on the Pool, when they came into unpleasant proximity to a huge croc', as we called the reptile. He extended his frightful jaws in an alarming manner; but one well-directed bullet put into his scaly body caused him to dive into the depths. On the afternoon of our second day from the Pool, a dreadful storm came up, and we were tossed about as though we were at sea. With some difficulty we came to a bank, where we secured our steamer to a tree, and dropped anchor for the night. While we were at supper in our cabin, a hippo' came and paid us a visit. He floundered and spouted around for a time, and finally departed. Again and again we saw natives on the south bank, looking at us with evident interest. Many of them do not yet feel sure that our smoke boat is a thing without life. If it has no life, how does it make that noise? Where does all that white smoke come from? Where are they putting all that wood?

When about three hours from Kua Mouth, our steamer got into rough water. There was a powerful current on our starboard side, with a tremendous whirlpool directly in front of us. Had we known this in time, we might have avoided the full force of it. It must be remembered that even now, the river is not fully known, and many dangers have yet to be discovered. At two in the afternoon we were approaching this dangerous point. I was feeling rather below par, and was standing on the starboard side of our cabin, and next to the south bank of the Congo. Mr. W. and a colored man were at the wheel, and Mr. B. was near the engines, aft. Our steamer made several rough movements, which caused me to look forward. In doing so, I saw the whirlpool and the strong current. At such a time and in such a current, it was too late to alter the course of our steamer with good effect. Into the whirlpool we went, and the current struck the starboard side where I was, turning the bow directly across the current. The steamer's starboard side went completely under. It seemed to me that nothing could save her from foundering. Believing that she would immediately go down, I made an effort to reach her port side, as, if I remained on the starboard, I would be under her in case she sunk. By the time I reached her port side,

L

with a great struggle, as though she knew she had precious freight on board, the little steamer righted herself, and I felt the danger was past. One of our boys had a narrow escape, and our colored helmsman was thrown upon the deck. Some fowls and cooking utensils were washed overboard, as also my clock, which was on the cabin. But we were safe. Had the steamer gone down, it would have been utterly impossible to swim ashore; the distance was too great, the current was too strong, and crocodiles were too numerous. We named this part of the river " Clock Point."

At Kua Mouth we made fast for the night. In the morning there was great commotion among the natives. A young native drank a lot of palm wine, fell into the water, and was seized by a crocodile. For hours the natives hunted along the banks in their canoes, hoping to find some trace of him, but without success. His poor mother came and sat on the shore by our steamer, and, assisted by her sympathizers, was loud in her lamentations. It was really painful to hear the poor old creature call for her boy, who could no longer be found. Kua Mouth was formerly a station of the Congo Free State, but it has since been turned over to the French Jesuit priests.

One day from Kua Mouth, we set our men to chop wood. This was by no means an easy task, as the jungle was very thick, and as our men penetrated the wood to search for dead timber, they had to cut their way with their hatchets. Here in this isolated spot we spent a rather pleasant night. When we got to a good sandy beach like this one, our men usually preferred to sleep on the sand, surrounded by camp fires. We slept on board. Here in spite of dangers from crocodiles, our boys enjoyed themselves in the water for half an hour. They are good swimmers and almost amphibious.

We started the next morning early. My readers would laugh to hear our men when they are heaving off the whale boat Sailor-like, or rather Zanzibari-like, one shouts:

"Elambra."

This is replied to by the others with, "a." They repeat this several times, upon which they unitedly shout as they heave:

"U-pra-a-a."

In these forests there is much wood that would be valuable if it could be readily transported to some market. As we passed, now and then monkeys took sly glances at us from the trees, which glances I returned. That is, I looked up cautiously, thinking they might take it into their head to throw some dead branches of a tree at me.

In the afternoon we called for half an hour at Bolobo, where was a station of the Congo Free State, but which had been recently abandoned. The south bank of the river at this point is densely populated, and we saw several thousand natives within the space of half an hour. The station of the Congo Free State was twice burned by the natives, but for what cause I could not ascertain. We found it difficult to purchase food at this point. The people retired sullenly from the bank as we approached, and each man was fully armed. The spectacle was appalling. The thought that these horrid-looking men and women, tatooed all over, and fantastically dressed, had never-dying souls, was an almost overwhelming one. Dressed, did I say? Many of them were as naked as when they were born. Most of them carry flint-lock guns, native knives, and long spears. Here, after a good deal of effort, we purchased " kwanga," peanuts, sugar-cane, fish, and corn. Our boys did a good trade in disposing of our empty meat tins, which, though worthless to us, were prized by the Bolobo. The boys traded off these tins with such shrewdness as would put many an English or American boy in the shade. These people on the Upper Congo are emphatically traders. With skill they will drive a bargain. I have wandered among the Indians of Wyoming and Montana. I have visited them in their "tepees" in order to obtain interesting "curios" from them. That the Sioux Indians are cunning, the pale-faced American knows too well; but for skill and cunning and artfulness in buying and selling, the Upper Congo trader surpasses the dusky inhabitants of the far West. Of course, some phases of their trading transactions are calculated to provoke a smile. One man approaches our whale boat in a small canoe, with a few large dried fish for sale. The Zanzibar men in the whale boat want the fish. The fish trader exhibits his specimens, but guardedly, and at a safe distance.

" Bring the fish," shout the Zanzibaris.

"Show the brass rods."

"Here they are; bring the fish closer. Hand them to us."

"No; you hand the brass rods first, and then I will give you the fish."

"You give us the fish first, and we will then give to you the brass rods."

After much talk the price of a particular fish is finally agreed upon; but how is the native to secure the brass rods? and how is the Zanzibari to make sure of the smoked fish?

The Zanzibari stretches toward the canoe; the native pulls a trifle nearer; both are now excited.

"Give me the fish."

"Give me the ten brass rods."

"Give me the fish first."

"Give me the ten brass rods first."

Both men are now close to each other. The native grasps one end of the brass rods, while the Zanzibari eagerly seizes the tail end of the fish.

"Let go the fish."

"Let go the brass rods."

Each man releases one, and grasps the other more

A Native Village.

tenaciously. The Zanzibari rejoices in his fish, and the Bolobo rejoices in his brass rods. The whole transaction was "malamu baa," or very good.

Mr. B., who was with me on the "Henry Reed," thus writes of a previous visit to this place, Bolobo.

"Soon after our arrival we heard tremendous drumming and shouting in the town. On inquiry we found some one had died. This led us to desire a walk into the towns, that we might get to know some of the habits and customs of the people. We went, and saw a most disgusting, pitiful, and heart-sickening sight. After passing through several villages, we came to an open space, where a great company of natives had assembled. The first thing to attract our attention was a large circle of men, who had been drinking palm wine till they were nearly drunk, and then were joining in a kind of savage dance, accompanied by wild singing and shouting. A little farther on we saw a still larger circle of women, who were smoking pipes about two feet in length, and at the same time, laughing, dancing, and shouting in a most hideous fashion.

"A little to the left of them, in the middle of a native hut whose wall had been removed, stood the coffin, containing the body of the departed, and it was surrounded by women mourners, some wives, and other friends of the dead; the whole formed such a sight that I shall never forget.

"We noticed that two of the women and one man of the party that surrounded the coffin had been stripped of their usually scanty clothing, and a few blades of green grass given as a substitute. We also saw that their hands were made fast by native rope. Oh, what a look they gave us as we approached! In answer to a question we were told 'these three are ready to be killed to celebrate the death of this chief.' Two of them were his wives, and the other was a slave."

Mr. B.'s description is but a faint picture of the awful doings of these Bolobos. When a chief dies, they believe that he goes into a spirit world, and that he should be accompanied by his wives and slaves. Hence the death of a popular chief causes much bloodshed. Their common mode of execution is as follows: The person chosen is securely fastened down to a rude chair, which is also tied to pegs driven into the ground. This chair is placed under a tree. A branch from the tree is forced downward, directly over the head of the condemned one. The branch is further secured to the head by means of cords made from the fibre of the palm. One well-directed blow with a knife, wielded by the strong arm of the executioner, and the bleeding head is thrown upward, as the branch returns to its position, and the body is afterward cast into the river.

Leaving Bolobo, we sailed for several hours, and then anchored alongside a sandbank. Here our men worked for several hours, getting a supply of firewood, after which we retired for the night. At midnight we were awakened by indications of a storm. Presently it came—the rains descended and the floods came, and the winds blew, and I had to envelop myself in my waterproof coat and overalls. Thus I slept the remainder of the night. Next day the captain and myself shot at a number of "hippos." We did not, however, stop the steamer to wait and see how far we had been successful.

That evening we were again favored with a fine sandy beach, where we made fast for the night. But alas! it seemed as though the mosquitoes were specially arrayed to attack us. They stuck their proboscides into my face and hands with terrible effect. Here our boys shot a fine fish eagle and a pigeon. We had six fires on the bank, and all our men were busily engaged chopping wood. The tall trees a few yards away; the occasional screech of a nocturnal bird; the camp fires on the bank; the half-naked forms of our men, as they were cleaving wood; and the peculiar noise of our Zanzibaris with every stroke of the axe, and cut of the saw, made a weird scene. On the morrow we passed a number of large canoes going down the river. They were evidently cannibals, and came from above Lukolela. Indeed, cannibals in these regions are by no means rare. What a shudder it gives one to look upon the tatooed face of one who has many times feasted upon human flesh! One of the little steamers on the upper river was at one time in the interior. As it lay at anchor one evening, a young man connected with the steamer thought he would like to venture on shore, to see, and, if possible, converse with the strange people. To think was to act. He went and was soon surrounded by the natives, who had been watching the smoke boat with evident curiosity. Whatever their desires or intentions may have been, they were not openly hostile; but something in their attitude filled him with suspicion. Unfortunately, he could not understand their dialect. They were a strange people, and they therefore spake a strange tongue.

Several of them seized him by the fleshy part of his arm in a loving manner, and he distinctly heard the words, "Nyama bāā." His suspicions were aroused, and he made for his place of refuge, the steamer. They evidently desired to taste a little of the stranger's flesh, for our friend soon discovered that " nyama bāā " means plenty of meat.

It is most interesting to hear the natives shout to each other over the water. By necessity and a long experience, they have acquired the art of carrying on a conversation when at a great distance from each other. I can hardly imitate them on paper.

Arriving at Lukolela, we put up for the night. That is, we moored our steamer to some trees, and lit watch fires on the bank. At some stopping places it is very necessary to put two men to keep watch all night, to provide against an attack by the natives. This in many parts is now becoming less necessary.

When two men act as watchers, in order to insure their keeping awake, it is customary to make them shout to each other every half minute through the night. Often when disturbed by mosquitoes at midnight, I have heard the sonorous voices of the watchers, coming from different directions, beyond the camp fires, "W-a-t-c-h! W-a-t-c-h!"

Lukolela was formerly occupied by the Congo Free State, but only temporarily. The English Baptists have since established a mission there. While here, we saw some fine monkeys of a large species, and here, too, our boys shot some fine guinea fowl. Soon after blowing the whistle, our steamer was surrounded by natives in canoes, bringing "besumbu," or cassava for our men and boys, and fowls for us. Most of the people are of the Ba-yanzi tribe, and speak the Ki-yanzi language. Several of the women who brought food for us were tatooed all over their shoulders and arms, and the collars they wore must have been uncomfortable in the extreme. They were not made of paper or of linen, but of solid brass, varying in weight from ten to twenty-eight pounds. It is considered an honor to wear a large heavy brass collar, although it must surely be very distressing. Often have I met persons holding the collar with both hands, so as to relieve the throat and shoulders somewhat. This is never taken off until the wearers die, or until they are executed over the grave of their chief.

Of the fish offered for sale, we bought about one hundred, varying in weight from six to thirty-five pounds.

When the Congo Free State occupied this place temporarily, two white men were placed there. Both spent much of their time in hunting " hippos," crocodiles, elephants, and buffaloes. One fatal day they were charged by a buffalo bull, and one of the white men was killed. The other escaped by climbing a tree. Mr. G., who escaped, was personally known to me, and we spent many an hour together at the Equator Station.

The following evening after leaving Lukolela, we anchored hard by another sandbank. Our camping place was beautiful for situation. The sand when in the water looked like gold dust, and I was reminded of Bishop Heber's hymn:

"Where Afric's sunny fountains
Roll down their golden sand."

But "All is not gold that glitters": there is probably no gold in this sand.

Here, myself, Mr. W., Captain Masari, and Mr. B. became children once more, and joined our boys right heartily in a game of leap-frog on the sands. During the night we had another real tropical storm. Mr. W., being on the exposed side, was drenched, bed clothes and all, and he had to seek shelter in the cabin, to be tormented, alas! by mosquitoes. The wind blew furiously, but I obstinately refused to get up, or rather get down, for I was perched on the cabin.

Morning came. Joy came with the morning. The clouds dried their tears; the winds sank to rest, and our men finished their wood chopping.

# CHAPTER XVII.

EQUATOR STATION—"BUY ME, INGILEZA"—CURIOUS QUESTIONS
—ARE THEY MAKING SOUP—OH, THY POCKET IS EMPTY—A VISIT
FROM SAVAGES—SHUT YOUR EYES.

AMONG those who came to visit the white man's place at Equator Station was a stalwart young man from the town of Wangata. He had a fine physique, and his features were almost handsome. Though his breast was tatooed, his face was without a mark, save two large lumps of flesh in front of his ears. In order to cause these lumps, the flesh must have been greatly strained and lacerated. They stood out so prominently as to almost hide his ears, and gave to him a peculiar appearance. These marks probably distinguished him as a slave among the people from whom he came. He was still a slave, and owned by old Ipambi, one of the chiefs of Wangata, and who was also the executioner of the district. I can hardly describe Ipambi. He was more like a fierce animal than a man. While trading up the "Ikilemba," he purchased Bana Ngulu. Ipambi owned several other slaves, though they had no particular work, and neither were they fed by him. They had to get their food as best they could. According to custom, these slaves would be killed over Ipambi's grave, so that their spirits might accompany him to the other world. These poor slaves, unless they should happen to die, can only look forward to the time when their blood will be shed over their master's grave. This custom prevails in nearly the whole of Central Africa. Dr. Wolf, who explored the Sankuru, and whom I met at Banza Manteke, reports that when the old king of Lukengo died, one thousand unfortunate wives and slaves were slaughtered on his grave. Bana Ngulu had, no doubt, often witnessed these awful and bloody scenes. He would not look upon them as we do. He would probably feel that such an end was almost inevitable, and that his master had absolute control over him. Like the cloth and brass rods, the sheep and goats, he formed part of his master's wealth.

As soon as I was able, I spoke to Bana Ngulu. My name up here was Plobela, which I adapted from Probert, as this they could not utter. They find a great difficulty in pronouncing the letter R. My brother's name was Mr. E. He was known as Ngileza, probably altered by some one from the word English. Bana Ngulu would stand outside, opposite the porch, and say:

"Bondele, buy me; I would like to work."

"What can you do, Bana Ngulu?"

"Let me go with your men to cut sticks."

"Well, we will try and agree with Ipambi about your wages."

Ipambi was willing to have Bana Ngulu work for us. Bana Ngulu received his food, and Ipambi got the pay. About this time Bana Ngulu became apprehensive that Ipambi was about to kill him for some reason. Each time he returned with his load of wood, he would say so eagerly:

"Bondele, buy me. I'll work so hard for you. I won't run away. Buy me, Bondele, and send me to Kintamo. I am afraid Ipambi is going to kill me."

And so he begged, earnestly but respectfully, every chance he had. We had become so interested in Bana Ngulu, that we really wanted to liberate him from the

M

power of that miserable tyrant, Ipambi. It had to be managed with the greatest care, as Ipambi would ask a very high sum if he knew we were anxious to buy. Mr. G., of the English Baptist Mission, wanted the man to work at Stanley Pool, and was willing to give a good sum for him. After a good deal of talk with Ipambi, as is customary in all trading transactions, Ipambi agreed to sell his man for eight hundred brass rods and a few other articles. With his usual shrewdness, Ipambi said:

"Bòndele, I won't take the pay now. If I do, the people will see me carrying it. When the sun is gone down, and it is quite dark, I will come."

"All right, Ipambi."

At eight in the evening he came, with a slave to assist him in carrying his money. We counted out for him his brass rods; and in addition to these, we gave him one small mirror, a knife, spoons, and a tin plate. The total cost of ransoming Bana Ngulu was less than sixteen dollars. Poor Bana did not dream of freedom; he simply wanted a master with whom his life would be safe. It was some time before he could realize that he was not bought, but liberated.

The missionary or traveler who goes to Africa must be prepared to hear, if not to answer, some very strange, curious questions. Many questions are asked that the missionary could easily answer in his own tongue; but to reply in the language of the native is a very different thing. Then some questions are asked which it would be difficult to answer in any language; while others are simply amusing. I once went with Mr. B. to visit a certain town. The old chief sat upon a log, sharpening his knife, while he and his people listened to the strange words. Mr. B. was saying something about the other world, when the chief interrupted:

"How am I going to get up there? (Pointing to the clouds). How could I return?" For he had no idea of remaining in the other world. All this was asked in sober earnestness.

At Banza Manteke, when Mr. R. was speaking to the people, he was asked, what seemed to them a very practical question:

"Can not our women work on the day you call 'Lumingu' (Sunday)?

The first time white men appeared on the Upper Congo, many funny questions were asked.

"Are those things fast on his face?" (The spectacles.)

"Did those things grow on his feet?"

The first steamers caused no little surprise.

"Look at that smoke boat."

"What makes it move through the water faster than our canoes?"

"What is that man doing (the fireman) putting sticks in that hole?"

"What makes that noise?"

"Look at that white smoke."

"Are they making soup?"

Down country some of our people were asked:

"How do you make your cloth so pretty?"

"Can white people make food from earth?"

One day, while talking in a distant town, one of our missionaries was asked:

"Who made God?"

"Who is the stronger, God or the devil?"

"If God is so strong, why does he not prevent the devil from tempting us?"

Once at Mukimvika, one of the missionaries was asked:

"Will God die?"

" Has he a house?"

Some of these questions serve to show how much these poor people need the light. They also remind us of an English missionary in another part of Africa. He was speaking to the natives of the great country from which he came, and of the noble queen who ruled it, when he was interrupted with " How many cows has your queen got?"

What corresponds to our letter "O" is largely used by the Balolo tribe who live on and near the Equator. Let me here explain the " Ba" and the " Ki" used by nearly all the tribes of the great Bantu race. " Ba and Ki are prefixes. The one means the people, the other the language. For example, " Ba-lolo" means the people, a certain tribe ; " Ki-lolo " means the language spoken by that tribe.

As to the "O," a brief conversation would be as follows :

" White man."

" O ? "

" Health to you."

" O, health to you."

" Where are you going?"

"O, I am going into the town."

Or the native may be leaving the station for home.

"Eanga." (Name of a friendly fisherman.)

"O?"

"You are going in the road?"

"O, you stay?"

"O."

The Balolo have many peculiar expressions. Sometimes after a man has made a purchase, and is about to sell the article to another, the first owner may feel inclined to interfere. This is objected to. If he insists, he is met with—

"Would you sell the axe again?"

The meaning is, "You have sold a thing. Have you anything further to do with it?"

No Balolo man wishes to be reminded of his poverty. Perhaps that is true of the human race. But the Balolo native likes to think he is rich. It is offensive to call any one poor. Two natives may have a hot dispute. The one says very hard things, but the other gives him a deadly thrust, by saying:

"Thy pocket sounds empty; mine full."

This pocket is a kind of bag, in which they carry

their money, such as cowries and brass rods. It is usually suspended from the shoulder.

The children in our mission attach great importance to closing the eyes during prayer. In our own land I have observed a want of reverence in this respect, and have often wished that we might learn a lesson even from our little Congo children. I am not sure, however, that they are altogether prompted by feelings of profound reverence. Sometimes the tired little things will fall asleep at prayers in the evening.

One of our missionaries once visited a strange town, and after speaking to the people, desired them to close their eyes, while he prayed to God. His request had a moving effect, for during prayer nearly all the people beat a hasty retreat. Alas, poor creatures! how did they know what harm might come upon them while their eyes were closed! While at the Equator among the Balolo, we were visited by people who lived several days distant. They came to buy cloth, knives, spoons, looking glasses, brass nails, for which they offered fowls, sheep, and goats.

One morning quite a large number of these savages came to the station—frightful-looking fellows they were. Their hair was dressed in a fantastic manner; their bodies were smeared with grease and sprinkled with red powder; their faces decorated with streaks of yellow and white clay, and each one carried a knife, spear, or gun. We induced them to attend our morning service, which was held for half an hour in one of our large rooms. Partly out of curiosity they came. Each man brought his arms, and stood in the back part of the room. When Mr. E. was about to offer prayer, our Balolo boys turned to these men, and said, in a severe whisper:

"Komba baishu bakinyu" (shut your eyes).

They did close their eyes, and placed one hand tightly over them, while with the other they held their arms. I did not close my eyes, but peeped through my fingers to observe the effect upon the strangers. There was a fierce whisper, then a movement, and the man next the door was soon on the outside, followed by his companions. In a stooping position they ran, with a hand still pressed on their closed eyes, nor did they open them until they were fifty yards from the door.

# CHAPTER XVIII.

WOMAN STEALERS—WADZ' OKUM—WHO IS THE GREATEST—
LONGEST ARMS—KILOLO HYMN—CLOSING ARTICLE—LIGHT
FOR ETHIOPIA.

ONE night at the Equator, when our men were seated around the watch fire they discerned a canoe with several natives attempting to pass in silence along the back current. They were evidently strangers, for had they known our new place, they would have rowed against the current in mid stream, as the river is very wide.

"Why do ye not sing?" shouted our men.

"Speak," they shouted, "if you are peaceable people. Whence come you, and whither go you thus in silence?"

The occupants of the canoe pulled harder, but made no reply, upon which our men, before we could prevent them, seized large firebrands and threw them at the canoe. With some difficulty we made them desist, and the canoe passed on without any remonstrance from its silent oarsmen. This really looked suspicious, and we felt there was some ground for the remark of our boys:

"Iyo bantu baubi" (they are bad people).

We soon forgot all about it, and went to rest. At daybreak next morning, we were aroused by hearing men, women, and children making most unearthly noises, each one trying to speak louder than the rest. All the men were armed, some with flint-lock guns, or knives; others with spears and shields, or bows and arrows. My first thought was, "They are going to attack us," as I distinctly heard the words, "Kundel' iyo" (shoot them). We were speedily relieved by finding that they did not offer any violence to our persons, when we appeared on the veranda. On all sides were heard shouts of:

"Oh, mundele, yaka ndanza, kundel' iyo la umbau oke" (Oh, white man, come outside, shoot them with your gun).

We said, "Ipambi, what is the matter?"

"Look, look!" said he, pointing out upon the river, where I observed a canoe going swiftly down the current. I called for my glass, and saw there were three men and one woman in the canoe.

I asked, "Who is that woman?"

"Wadz' okum," shouted a man near me, and who was in great distress; "Wadz' okum, white man" (my wife, white man). They wanted us to shoot, either because they knew our Winchesters would carry farther, or because they had greater confidence in our skill as marksmen; but we did not oblige them.

"Ipambi, we must not shoot, but we are sorry for you. We come not here to kill, for we love you all. Unless you pursue them, we can not help you. We come from a land many days distant, to tell you how to do right. You often steal people, and you have killed many with that big knife by your side. You steal from each other; you kill each other; it is all wrong, but tell us how this happened."

"I will, mundele. Last night a canoe came to the bank of the river, opposite our town, and we knew it not. Early this morning the wife of this man went to the river to fetch water, and was seized and carried off as you have seen."

"Be prepared if they come again, and know, Ipambi, we are your friends if you do right."

"Oh, yes, mundele, we know that."

And so they retired to their town, one mourning the loss of his wife, whom he would never see again. Whether she was sacrificed at some cannibal feast, or sold as a slave, or became the wife of a chief of a far-off tribe, we had no means of finding out.

Upper Congo natives have their ideas of superiority as have the other tribes and nations. The roads in Congo are narrow, not wide enough for two to go abreast. On the Lower Congo, this road is called "njila"; among the Balolo it is called "mboka." One day I went to a certain town with a friend who had been there before, and naturally he took the lead. The natives in the town asked:

"Why do you go in front of the other white man?"

"Because I know the road."

"But the other white man has the longest whiskers."

They could not understand how men could be equal in office and position. Once we were asked:

"Why do you not fight and see who is the better man, then let him be chief?"

"No; that would be wrong and foolish. We do not want to be chief.

One instance may be given to show that the Bayanzi and Balolo traders have considerable tact and shrewdness. They frequently came to our station to buy our cloth. We usually sold our cloth by the fathom. On the table, in front of the store window, we had marks to indicate various lengths. The table itself would measure just six feet, or as a Balolo man would say, "Loboko lo monkolo." Six feet or one fathom is about as much as a person can stretch with his arms. Sometimes a number of traders would come at one time, and they would want to measure the cloth themselves. We could not at first guess the reason of this. Did they suspect us? No, it could not be that. Did they fear we gave them short measure? They knew better than that. They wanted to be permitted to measure cloth, so that they might select the man with the longest arm, and thus gain a few inches on each fathom.

1 here give my readers a verse of a hymn in the Kilolo language. It was composed by one of our American Baptist Mission Union missionaries, during my residence at Wangata, and the full translation is below.

Nzakomba O Fafa;
We mongo ndemaki;
Toma toe tomumu,
We kika le bolemi.

God our Father;
Thou thyself didst make me;
Of all things
Thou alone art the maker.

In the beginning, Father,
Thou didst make people;
Thou didst give them spirits;
They understood thy words.

Our bodies
Will die, but
For ever and for ever (season by season)
Our spirits will live (or have life).

It was midnight. I was traveling up the country. My bed was fixed. The grass was the carpet; the sky was the ceiling. Hearing a noise near the camp, and wishing to ascertain what it was, I arose, struck a match, applied it to the candle in the lantern, and the light dispelled the darkness which a moment before surrounded me. As I returned to my bed, I thought: "Africa has been enveloped for ages in great moral and spiritual darkness. As the only way to dispel natural darkness is to introduce light, so the only way to dispel the gross darkness that hangs over that vast continent, like some deathly nightshade, is to introduce the light of 'the glorious gospel of the blessed God'; to tell them of him who said: 'I am the Light of the world.' Shall we, then, heed the cry from Macedonia? Shall not those who now sit in darkness hear of the world's Redeemer? Shall we hide from the regions beyond the glorious gospel of Christ, which is our joy in life, and our only hope in death?"

Let the memories of those who have fallen in the conflict inspire us with holy zeal. All may not actually go out, but all may render some assistance. If you cannot descend the mine, hold the ropes. The time for seed-sowing is short. The king's business requireth haste. "Men of Israel, help." The midnight darkness of the "dark continent" is slowly, but surely passing away. The morning cometh. The time of Afric's visitation is come. Ethiopia shall soon stretch out her hands in supplication unto a loving and pardoning God.

"From Congo's mighty river,
  And densely-peopled plains,
They call us to deliver
  Their souls from Satan's chains.
A land of beauteous sunshine,
  Fairer than Ceylon's isle ;
Where every prospect pleases—
  But man, poor man, is vile.

"Winds do not waft the gospel,
  Nor waves the message roll ;
The sweet and 'old, old story,'
  Must fill the human soul.
Souls by the Lord appointed,
  Who all things count but loss ;
Men for the work anointed,
  Whose glory is the cross.

"Light of this world's gross darkness,
  On Ethiopia shine,
Till Ham's sin-stricken children
  Receive the beams divine.
Thou Light of earth's dark pathway,
  Light of the world above ;
Guide Afric's sons and daughters
  To heaven, where all is love."


THE END.

www.ingramcontent.com/pod-product-compliance
Lightning Source LLC
Chambersburg PA
CBHW021727220426
43662CB00008B/742